PRACTICAL SIGIL MAGIC FOR BEGINNERS

PRACTICAL SIGIL MAGIC

FOR BEGINNERS

A GUIDE TO Setting Intentions,
Crafting Powerful Symbols,
and Applying Spells

Shannon C. Clark
Illustrations by Jacinta Kay

ROCKRIDGE
PRESS

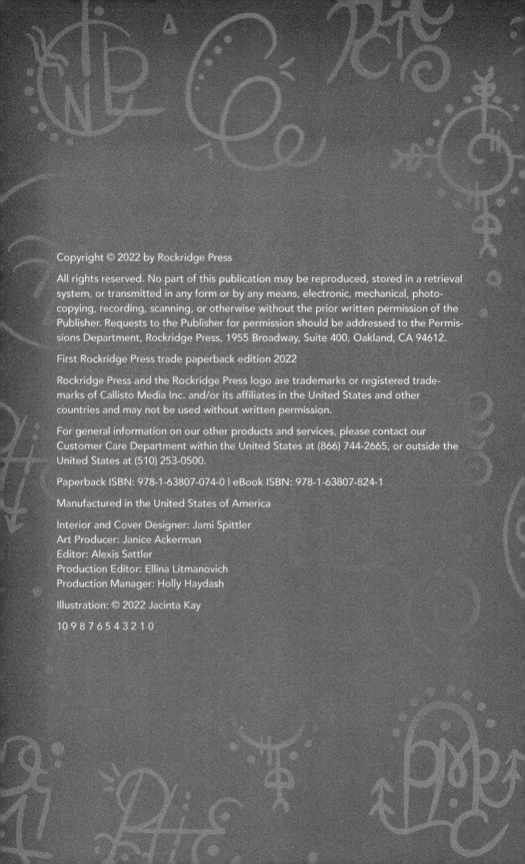

First Rockridge Press trade paperback edition 2022

Rockridge Press and the Rockridge Press logo are trademarks or registered trademarks of Callisto Media Inc. and/or its affiliates in the United States and other countries and may not be used without written permission.

For general information on our other products and services, please contact our Customer Care Department within the United States at (866) 744-2665, or outside the United States at (510) 253-0500.

Paperback ISBN: 978-1-63807-074-0 | eBook ISBN: 978-1-63807-824-1

Manufactured in the United States of America

Interior and Cover Designer: Jami Spittler
Art Producer: Janice Ackerman
Editor: Alexis Sattler
Production Editor: Ellina Litmanovich
Production Manager: Holly Haydash

Illustration: © 2022 Jacinta Kay

10 9 8 7 6 5 4 3 2 1 0

DEDICATED TO
ALL OF THOSE WHO SEEK
TO CREATE A LIFE FILLED
WITH MAGIC

CONTENTS

INTRODUCTION

Welcome to *Practical Sigil Magic for Beginners*. This book is written with beginners in mind, but anyone who has an interest in sigil magic can find something useful in its pages. Whether you have been a decades-long practicing witch or are looking to create a newly magical lifestyle, you're in the right place.

A sigil is a powerful drawn symbol that represents an idea or intention statement, which is a focused declaration of a goal or desire. Once activated, that symbol then speaks directly to your subconscious and launches your intention out to the universe. In fact, sigils work with every type of magic user because of their unique way of working with your subconscious. Sigils and symbols have been around for as long as humans have depicted thoughts through images. They tap into the part of our subconscious that reaches back for millennia into the power of our ancestors and the magic that they used. By transforming your idea or intention into a sigil, you are connecting history with your desire to create your future.

I started learning about sigils in 1994, when I first enrolled in a six-week class on ceremonial magic. I'd only recently found that magic was not just the stuff of fantasy books; I felt fascinated and completely called to it. During the last session, our group decided that we wanted to learn more and asked to meet again the next week. This same group then proceeded to meet for two more years, each week learning the basics of magic, astrology, tarot, herbs, oils, crystals, and, yes, sigils.

I immersed myself, spending every day doing the rituals exactly as I'd been taught, and used the precise candles, incense, herbs, oils, and crystals. This structure and dedication served me very well for many years, even after the class ended. Yet over time, I learned that in order to live a truly magical lifestyle, I needed to practice in a way that fit my own energy, personality, and habits. My daily life called for a different approach to magic than what I had been doing from the beginning. That's how I eventually came back around to using sigils in almost every aspect of my craft. They are compatible with any type of magic or lifestyle. They are adaptable; can be created quickly, with some practice; and with only a few basic tools, they are quite effective. I once placed a hidden sigil for truth in my office. Beginning the next day, I started finding out some truths about the people I was working with. Then some larger truths began unfolding about my bosses, which ultimately led me to resign. I have come to see how powerful sigils are, and I hope that sharing what I know might just make a difference for other people, too.

This book was written to inspire you to practice a form of magic that is in alignment with your unique values, regardless of your background, experience, magical affiliation, religious denomination, or spiritual path. While this magic is very effective, the most important part of your journey is that you *love* what you're doing.

HOW TO
USE THIS BOOK

In PART I: THE WONDERS OF SIGILS, you'll discover the ancient origins of sigils and their evolution into today's world. You'll learn about readying yourself for rituals, preparing a sacred space, celestial timing, the pros and cons of using your own sigils versus someone else's, creating your own sigils, activating sigils, and incorporating sigils into your daily routines.

You'll also learn how to create powerful intention statements that leave no room for misinterpretation.

In PART II: UNLEASH YOUR SIGIL MAGIC, you'll find a collection of spells to practice. Each one lists the required and optional tools and ingredients, how much time it should take to perform, and step-by-step instructions.

You might be tempted to skip right to the spells in this book, but I encourage you to start at the beginning and to look closely at the guidelines at the beginning of Unleash Your Sigil Magic (page 49) so that you gain a thorough understanding of the fundamentals. This will help you perform the spells with the respect, power, and confidence that you need in order to produce optimal results.

Magic of every kind requires the utmost respect. The care and effort you put into each ingredient, step, and intention is the energy that empowers it. Everything is energy, and the energy you direct at an object affects that object. Honor and gratitude enhance any object's power, while disrespect and apathy will only disempower it.

Sigil magic is a powerful tool in your arsenal for transformation, and like anything else, it requires understanding, patience, dedication, and even some trial and error to get it right. Be patient with yourself, learn and practice at your own pace, and enjoy the journey.

PART I

THE WONDERS OF SIGILS

This part of the book will take you on a deep dive into the what, where, how, and why behind sigil magic. You'll learn to differentiate between a sigil, talisman, and symbol. And you'll be able to spot the connections between sigils and other forms of magic.

Chapters 1 and 2 explore how sigils can help you find your own magical style and manifest your distinct intentions. In particular, you'll learn how to create powerful intention statements that leave no room for misinterpretation. You'll discover safe and mindful approaches to prevent unintended results.

This part of the book also presents different ways to engage in rituals, including preparing your mind, body, and sacred space for practicing magic, and selecting appropriate tools and ingredients. From there, you'll try different ways to activate a spell. You'll even get a chance to create your first sigil. With this groundwork, you'll be able to start practicing your craft with confidence and power.

CHAPTER 1

An Introduction to Sigil Magic

Sigils, in many ways, are like enhanced positive affirmations. The difference is that a sigil is formed as an image that is easier for the subconscious to understand, and the intention statement used to create it might be more meticulously worded than a positive affirmation is. This specific and focused approach to working with magical energy will help you reach results that are consistent over time. After all, you're not here to practice "accidental" magic.

This chapter covers the fundamentals of sigils. You'll gain a deeper understanding of not only why they work but also how they work. The more you understand the basics, the easier it will be to create sigils, work with them, and incorporate them into your daily life. You'll discover that they work with every kind of magic, such as nature magic, ceremonial magic, witchcraft, candle magic, tarot, and any other kind of magic you might imagine. This is part of what makes sigil magic unique: It works with your preferences.

What Is a Sigil?

A sigil is a drawn creation that combines symbols, letters, dots, circles, lines, and other shapes into a single image that represents a specific idea or intention that you would like to manifest. It is a visual element connecting your conscious awareness—where your will, focus, and intentions reside—to your subconscious and the universal flow of energy.

A sigil can be drawn in any style that comes from your intuition: flowing, geometric, symmetrical, or asymmetrical. You do not need to be an artist; it doesn't matter so much what a sigil looks like, as long as all of your intention's energy has gone into its creation. It is not, however, a random squiggle drawing or a jumble of words thrown together.

A sigil is a symbolic representation of your intention, your statement of a goal or desire. Your intention is something you are committed to and willing to back up with action. It is worded as if it's already happened, distinct from a general wish or hope, to give the subconscious mind and the universe a way to see it as real *now*. The theory goes that if the mind believes your statement to be a current reality, this will allow for any blockages or filters in the subconscious to dissolve. For sigil magic, these statements are transformed into an image, because it is said that the subconscious understands images better than words.

Sigil magic itself actually refers to the *activation* of the sigil, rather than the creation of it. Chapter 2 goes into detail on many forms of activation, but for now just know that activation is the part of the process that gets the energy moving and flowing.

You might notice that some use the term "seals" when talking about sigils. Although the word "sigil" originates in the Latin *sigillum*, which means "seal," the magical use of the term today is slightly different. The modern distinction between "seal" and "sigil" is that *seals* are created to have influence over an entity that already exists, such as an angel or spirit, while *sigils* are an energetic extension of you and hold no command over other entities.

THE DIFFERENCE BETWEEN A SIGIL AND A TALISMAN

Another term that sometimes gets used interchangeably with "sigil" is "talisman." The difference between these two terms is that a talisman is an object, such as a pendant, ring, or charm, that has been made from a seal, sigil, or any other image that represents a specific energy. Sigils and seals can both be made into talismans so that you have an object to carry around with you in your pocket, wallet, or purse or to wear as jewelry. In fact, one way to activate a sigil that you have created is to turn it into a talisman if you have that skill. Usually, you will see talismans for protection and luck, but there are many others as well.

Some talismans are not made from sigils or seals at all. For instance, someone may have a four-leaf-clover charm that they carry for luck. You can see there is no sigil or seal involved, but the talisman works because of the power of the agreed-upon meaning. In other words, at one point in time, someone thought that finding a four-leaf clover was lucky. That belief spread and is now known in many cultures. There is an exponential increase in the amount and longevity of a specific energy when enough people are unified in a belief or thought pattern about it. The purpose of a talisman is to carry with you the energy that it represents, to help your subconscious shift perspectives when you feel disempowered.

The Origins of Sigil Magic

Sigil creation dates back to humankind's ancient beginnings. Some believe that our ancestors drew images on cave walls not only to tell stories of the past and present but also to bring about change for the future. An image of a person successfully stalking an animal could have been intended to bring luck in the upcoming hunt. This idea is referred to as "sympathetic magic."

As people evolved, they created markings that were more involved, complex, and varied. They drew images that represented their daily lives. These eventually became written languages, such as the hieroglyphics of ancient Egyptians or the fundamental logographic writing still used in China today.

At the same time, seals and sigils became more complex both in their visual elements and in their meanings. But they evolved along a different path than written language because they served a different objective. While written language has generally been intended for communication, sigils and seals are most often used to create change. It's a subtle difference, and one that leaves room for cross-purposes or purposes that overlap. Sometimes written language can be distilled down to its component images and, when done in conjunction with a focused intention, it yields a sigil.

Important Figures in Sigil History

Perhaps the best-known occultists to study classical sigils are Henry Cornelius Agrippa (b. 1486) and John Dee (b. 1527). Agrippa wrote *De Occulta Philosophia Libri Tres*, or *Three Books of Occult Philosophy*, a treatise on the magical arts that included the creation and purpose of sigils and seals. This tome is still studied as an instructional and philosophical resource today.

John Dee was also a prolific practitioner and, along with his assistant Edward Kelley, created a working version of *The Sigil of Ameth*, also called *Sigillum Dei,* meaning Seal of God, or *Signum Dei Vivi,* symbol of the living God. The first mention of this sigil predates their work and can be found in manuscripts from the 1300s. But Dee and Kelley's version is still used today by practitioners of ceremonial magic, as a way to keep falsehood away from their divinations.

THE IMPACT OF CHAOS MAGIC ON SIGIL MAGIC

Chaos magic is a modern practice that was founded in England in the 1970s by Peter J. Carroll and Ray Sherwin. It is based on Austin Osman Spare's sigil philosophy. Carroll, Sherwin, and others originated the method as a way to practice magic without dogma, religion, or any outside mystical influence. They were focused on what could be called "mind magic," the energy used by which originates entirely from the practitioner. These results were seen as physical in nature rather than philosophical, moral, or spiritual. Sigil magic became a large part of chaos magic.

Because the goal of chaos magic is to produce a tangible effect, it encourages people to experiment with their magic and prioritize their instincts over rules or theories from classical magic. The thinking goes that if all the energy behind your magic comes from you rather than an outside source, like with sigil drawing and activation, then the method for channeling must be adapted to suit your unique energy.

The most important tenet in chaos magic is that a magic user's *belief* is what produces the results. If you believe wholeheartedly that what you're doing will work, then it will work.

The Relationship between Sigils and Other Forms of Magic

These days, sigil work has evolved to incorporate all kinds of magical practice, spell crafting, and philosophy. Many still practice under the label of "chaos magic," but it really isn't necessary for you to do so in order to use sigil magic. In fact, you can use sigil magic without labeling yourself or your beliefs at all.

This is because of the versatility of sigils. Their magic can be practiced alone using only pen and paper, or by just drawing a sigil in the air. Still, adding other forms of magical tools and practices, such as candles, herbs, oils, crystals, tarot, astrology, cleansing, banishing, and so on, will enhance, and perhaps speed up, the results that you'd like to produce. This is a choice you get to make based on your lifestyle, your energy, and your likes and dislikes. If you would rather not use a candle, for example, then don't; if incense is uncomfortable for you, then you can opt for a room spray instead, or nothing at all. The possibilities are endless.

The more that you learn about all kinds of magic, the more you will be able to expand your practice of sigil magic, creating your own spells and producing amazing results. Feel free to explore all the possibilities in every kind of magic, because they will help you discover what speaks to *you*.

The Distinctive Power of Sigils

If you begin with the belief that everything is energy, then the practice of magic is when your will moves and transforms that energy to produce a specific result. Within this understanding, sigil magic is a powerful tool because it removes the limitation of your conscious mind from the equation. The conscious mind can limit energy flow because of filters, opinions, and other ideas we possess.

It's the same phenomenon that occurs when you focus on something so intently that everything else around you seems to fade away to the background or disappear altogether. Sigil magic does this as well, but at a greater speed and intensity, because words have already been translated into images and energy, the shared language of your subconscious and the universe. The magic that you perform on the sigil—called activation—releases your intention out to your subconscious and the universe, to begin transforming your reality into the one *you* intend.

Sigil magic is unique in that you are using your own energy, will, and desire without having to use the rules and philosophies of any other kind of magic, *unless you want to.* Here are several more benefits to bringing sigil magic into your craft, no matter your experience level or belief system.

CLARIFY YOUR INTENTIONS AND DESIRES

There is a difference between saying something vaguely, like "I wish I could do that someday," and saying something with intention and power, like "I am doing that now." The first statement doesn't call you into action, whereas the second statement does.

Because crafting a sigil involves transforming language into an image, it requires a specific intention statement, which can be a great way to practice clarifying and defining your desires. This encourages self-reflection and the habit of regularly asking yourself what you would like and need in a given moment or in your life generally.

This awareness, in turn, may even change the way you communicate everywhere. By understanding how to properly create an intention statement, you may also start to be more present to what you're saying as you're saying it. You'll be attuned to your communication in a way that may even enhance your relationships with others and with yourself.

CREATE MAGIC THAT IS UNIQUE
AND MEANINGFUL TO YOU

In most forms of classical magic, practitioners are encouraged to first study the rules and philosophies of that methodology before casting spells or performing rituals. This allows the magic user to be able to build up a certain respect for magic, as well as develop an informed point of view from which to create their own magical routines *within that system.*

By using sigils, you'll be able to create your own unique magic right away. You can start performing spells in conjunction with studying the foundations that are common to many forms of magic, without having to subscribe to any particular philosophy, in whole or even in part. You can create and practice your magic with your current viewpoints, and as you experiment with what works and doesn't work for you, you'll get to build on those perspectives.

This creates magic that is meaningful to *you*.

INCORPORATE YOUR PERSONAL SIGILS IN YOUR SPELL WORK

Incorporating personal sigils into your spell work can enhance most of your other rituals, because it makes what you're manifesting personal to you and no one else. Your spells will be more effective because they are in tune with your unique energy.

Modern spell work is written to be as inclusive to as many people as possible, catering to differing experience levels, tastes, and personalities. This is great, because it creates an opening for everyone who's interested to learn magic. You'll want to bring as much of yourself to your spell work as you can in order to achieve your carefully thought-out results.

As a bonus, you will also be able to make your spells mobile. You can create a sigil, activate it, and carry it with you in your pocket, in your wallet, inside your phone case, or anywhere really.

MAKE YOUR INTENTIONS KNOWN TO THE UNIVERSE

Sigil magic is akin to speaking to the universe in its own language. By transforming your desires and intentions into a sigil, then activating it, you are opening up a direct line of communication between yourself and the universe. Your statement is sent out through the image of a sigil, which ensures complete privacy while keeping the message clear.

At the same time you are communicating to the universe using the sigil, the sigil is also preparing your mind to receive from the universe. This creates an alignment or coherence. The universe shows you the opportunity, and now you can actually see it. Over time, and with practice, this exchange creates a life full of synchronicities and opportunities of which you can take advantage.

MINIMIZING NECESSARY TOOLS

What if you don't have access to all the tools and ingredients that another form of magic calls for? That's another benefit of sigil magic; all you need is the air in front of you and an image in your mind. This makes it a practice accessible to anyone, and easy to reach for in any setting. You still need the knowledge to create an intention statement, and a sigil-crafting method that you could perform in your head, but in a pinch, it works. If you are just beginning, though, use paper and pen so that you can see more clearly what you're drawing.

Because of the versatility of sigil magic, you can use as many or as few tools as you like without affecting the outcomes that you want to create in your magic.

The Practical Magic of Sigils

In stories, people often practice magic in a darkened room with a bubbling cauldron and fog, or in the middle of a meadow dancing naked under the full moon. These narratives often feature special ingredients like "eye of newt" or "toe of frog." These certainly sound more mysterious and out of reach than if you were to use their modern names: mustard seed and buttercup.

Although some do practice magic very successfully that way, mirroring these portrayals wouldn't be practical for most people. So this book is focused on methods that you can use in your everyday life without having to find your nearest forest or three-foot cauldron.

For magic to be truly practical, it should be performable anytime and anywhere. It should meet you where you are and fit your routine. In other words, you shouldn't have to sacrifice anything, except the odd bit of paper and the time that you'd like to spend learning and practicing your craft.

Among many other things, sigils can be easily incorporated into and used to enhance your mind, body, and spirit. They can help you improve relationships, heal yourself, and nourish your home.

TEND TO YOUR MIND, BODY, AND SPIRIT

If you ever find yourself feeling out of balance, crafting sigils can help reestablish the stability between your mind, body, and spirit. The sigils allow you to work on anything that your body might need to feel whole and full of vitality.

For instance, you can create a sigil to calm your mind, to help you find time to meditate, or to enhance your knowledge of any subject by augmenting your mental power or intuition. You can also craft sigils for emotional balance.

There are sigil spells designed to help you find the energy or time to exercise, to better tune in to your body's nutritional needs, and to get more healing sleep. You could also craft sigils that allow you more time to focus on your spirituality, or to bring in a teacher or other knowledge source that you never knew existed.

When working with mind, body, and spirit together, your magic becomes more powerful and fulfilling.

IMPROVE YOUR RELATIONSHIPS

One way that sigils can help you improve your relationships is by allowing you to reflect on what it is that you really want in a romance, friendship, partnership, or family connection. When you create a specific intention regarding the dynamics *between* you and another, you gain insight into what you want in the relationship and what you're already bringing to it. Likewise, you give the universe an opportunity to help you clarify your intentions even further. For example, suppose you craft a sigil with the intention of developing a romantic relationship. The universe may then help you gain further insight into what you desire by placing you in a position to witness aspects of others' relationships that inspire you.

EMBRACE HEALING AND PROTECTION

It isn't always possible to control internal or external environments, and walking through the world vulnerable and exposed can sometimes lead to physical or emotional hurt. This is where sigils come in. They help you become aware of these risks, protect yourself as best you can, and support your own healing. For example, you might craft a sigil for a speedy recovery, one that relieves stress, one that helps you break a habit, or one that could help lead you to the perfect method of healing for your unique situation.

You might also use sigil magic to take a more proactive approach to your health. You can use it to help you *receive* the healing energy you require by making you aware of any frames of mind that could be blocking that energy. It can also bring an awareness of when you might not be paying enough attention to your body's signals of imbalance.

STAY OPEN TO INSPIRATION AND ABUNDANCE

Crafting sigils for openness, possibility, inspiration, and abundance are all ways to manifest joy through opportunity and creation. Sometimes feelings of inspiration and abundance can be challenging to hold on to. One day you feel like nothing can stop you from receiving everything you desire, and then the next day you can't seem to get away from that internal message of scarcity.

Practicing sigil magic that delves into the mechanics of abundance requires some finesse, because you need to keep in mind that you can have an abundance of negativity, as well as joy. You can also find that you're experiencing too much of a good thing. Use care in crafting the intention statements here. One that says "I am experiencing an abundance of attention" could be interpreted as any kind of attention and in any amount, whereas "I am experiencing an abundance of positive, measured attention" is less open to misinterpretation.

DRAW STRENGTH FROM THE NATURAL WORLD

The process of creating a sigil grounds you in the natural world, because you are taking something from your mind or spirit and transforming it into a physical object. And in an even more concrete way, you can create sigils specifically designed to connect you with nature directly. For instance, you could craft a sigil that opens up the barriers between yourself and the earth. Or you could create one that allows you to find new ways to bond with nature to fill your spirit with the power of the natural world. Sigil magic like this is most effective when you actually use nature to activate the sigil. You might bury one under a bush or tree, or nest it in a potted plant indoors.

NOURISH YOUR HOME AND EVERYDAY LIFE

Sigils that are meant to be used in your everyday routines can be some of the most fun to create, because they're meant to enhance something concrete and present in your regular life. And you can place them anywhere you like so they will continue working once you've activated them. For example, you might create one to remind you to find joy in what's already available to you. Or you might perform sigil magic to keep in mind the value of putting in effort in certain areas of your life. You could even incorporate sigil magic with kitchen magic to create meals that nourish the spirit as well as the body. After all, an enchanted life begins with treasuring what you have and showing gratitude by working to keep it.

Sigil Magic Is Open to Anyone

The reason sigil magic is so potent is because of its accessibility, versatility, and adaptability. Anyone who has an interest in sigil magic can learn to do it successfully, whether it's your first time practicing magic or you've been practicing for decades. If you've been away from magic for a while or you've been dabbling here and there, sigil magic is an excellent way to get back into creating your magical life.

Because sigil magic is so straightforward, it can either stand on its own or be combined with any other kind of magic you feel called to. Its ability to produce results stems from its very long history of use. It's a forgiving form of magic as well. If you make an error, you can correct it and move on, or start again from the beginning, all with a minimum of unintended consequences.

While sigil magic is, at heart, a user-friendly form of magic, it still does require practice. Practice will allow for a more thorough understanding of why the magic works and why it might fizzle, thus leading to better results. It also requires patience, both with yourself so that you are not discouraged by mishaps, and with the spells themselves by giving them the *time* to work. With some diligence and focus, you could become an expert, creating sigils on the fly, or even performing magic completely in your mind.

Chapter 2 will delve into the steps and guiding principles you'll need to begin your own practice.

CHAPTER 2

The Basics of Creating Sigil Magic

You are now a scholar of sigil magic, having learned some of the history, context, and guiding principles of the craft. The path is entirely open for you to become a practitioner.

This chapter covers the how-to part of crafting sigils. In discovering the difference between symbols and sigils, you'll learn how to make one into the other. You'll see how to ground and center your mind, a crucial step before any magic work, and set a specific intention for your magic. The chapter then dives into the nitty-gritty of creating the dots, lines, and shapes that make up sigils and the various ways that you can create your own.

Once you have learned how to create a sigil, it is time to activate it. So, the next part of the chapter covers activation, as well as what to do with a sigil after activation. Chapter 2 winds down with a discussion of how to incorporate other magical systems into your sigil practice.

Turning a Symbol into a Sigil

It would be easy to mistake symbols for sigils, but there is a difference between the two.

A symbol is an image that represents an idea or object to a group of people. It often has an agreed-upon meaning and can be used to communicate or to provoke insight. Many times, a symbol and its significance are passed from generation to generation. An ankh symbol from Egyptian hieroglyphs, for example, is usually translated as "everlasting life" and has been found on Egyptian architecture dating back thousands of years.

A sigil, however, is created with a specific intention and can be made *from* symbols, increasing their complexity and forming an image that is precise and private.

Imagine a spiral, drawn alone as a symbol. It holds significance in cultures all over the world, including the ancient Celts, as a representation of "looking inward" or "following a path of spirituality." Those are very powerful concepts and, as a visual message, can inspire change in someone. But it is possible to use the spiral symbol and its meaning to craft something tailored to your own needs by adding the spiral to a sigil.

For example, you could craft a specific intention statement such as "I look inward to find my self-worth" or "I make time to follow my spiritual path each day." Then you may incorporate the spiral symbol along with other symbols, letters, lines, and dots that represent "self-worth" or "making time each day" to you. At the end, you'll have designed a sigil that specifically represents your intention. Only you, and the universe, will know its true meaning.

Ground Yourself and Center Your Mind

Preparation is the cornerstone of many magical traditions, including sigil work. Preparation for sigil work involves grounding and centering yourself, which clear a path for the magic to flow, link you with the energies that surround you, and enable your magic to use those sources as strength. More concretely, grounding and centering your mind entails taking some initial steps to clear your head and maintain your focus during a ritual. There are a few different ways to ground and center yourself: setting up for the ritual, connecting to your surroundings, and connecting to your body.

Sometimes, just gathering the tools and ingredients you need for a ritual or setting up your work space can create that sense of focus needed to clear your path before beginning sigil work.

Another way of grounding and centering is to connect to your surroundings. You might stand barefoot on grass, sit with your back against a tree, or do some gardening. You could close your eyes and listen to your space, smell the air, or look at the objects in your environment with presence and gratitude.

You can also center yourself by connecting to your body. Yoga, stretching, meditation, breathing, taking a sea-salt bath, and even mindfully drinking tea can serve the purpose of de-stressing, calming, eliminating distractions, and clearing your mind and heart. Now you have the perfect palette to start setting your intention.

Always Start by Setting an Intention

An intention statement is a focused declaration of a goal or desire that you have. It's worded as if it's already happened, to distinguish it from a general wish or hope, and to give the subconscious mind and the universe a way to see it as real right now. A clear intention statement gives the energy produced by your magic a direct path to follow, bringing you exactly what you desire. While each statement should be personal to you, there are some best practices to keep in mind as you start.

(o) WRITE IN THE PRESENT TENSE. Your subconscious operates from the present. So instead of saying "I will be confident," say "I am confident."

(o) AVOID THE PHRASE "I WANT . . ." Desire may be a powerful motivation, but it should not be mistaken for an outcome. To be, do, have, achieve, or experience is a more effective way to manifest a goal.

(o) KEEP IT POSITIVE. Try to emphasize what is (I am fearless), rather than what's missing (I'm not afraid anymore).

(o) BE REALISTIC IN YOUR DESIRE. Think about the intention "I am a lottery jackpot winner." There are two main problems with this statement. First, it leaves no room for everyday effort. Magic is fueled not just by mental focus but by energy that comes from actions. Second, it's restrictive. Magic operates in the realm of possibility. Offering one specific way to meet your need, such as winning the lottery, cuts magic off from other avenues that might serve you even better. So, a more effective intention statement might be "I live an abundant life, free from financial stress."

ⓦ WRITE ONLY ONE GOAL PER STATEMENT. Try to keep your statement to fifteen words or less to help avoid the temptation to load every desire you have into one sigil.

Transforming Dots, Lines, and Familiar Shapes

Sigils are drawn using lines, dots, shapes, letters, and other symbols. You'll see, or have perhaps already seen, ornate sigils and very simple ones. Some styles of sigil will resonate with some people and not others, but the power of a sigil has nothing to do with its beauty or how artistic its creator is.

That's good news, because it means that you don't have to have a single artistic molecule in your being to craft powerfully effective sigils. On the other hand, you could be an accomplished artist and make your sigils as complicated and lavish as you like. The power behind the sigil is in *the intention* that you infuse it with, and the strength of the sigil magic relies on the focus of the energy that you put into a sigil's activation, which you'll discover later in this chapter.

When you see a line, what does it mean *to you*? When you see a particular symbol, how does it make *you* feel? Do you love swirls and curls, or are you a fan of lines and symmetry? What you connect to is what's important. Keep working the sigil until it feels right to *you*. You don't need anyone else's opinion on how your sigil looks.

It all boils down to the specific and unique way that you combine all the lines, dots, and symbols. If it feels right to you, then it's perfect.

There Are a Variety of Methods for Creating Sigils

Some of the methods used in earlier centuries to craft sigils are impractical for today's magic users. They involved special tools and ingredients like virgin beeswax, the quill of a porcupine, or ink made from tree resin. That's because a sigil, prior to the 1970s, was created to have influence over a spirit or entity, rather than to reflect and pursue an intention statement. So, a practitioner would need to find as many objects as possible that correlated with the being in question, in order to enforce that connection.

Most methods that are popular today, however, prioritize intention statements to make goals clear. That way, if you don't believe in spirits and other outside influences, you have the control and you can still do magic. And while today's methods do still require time, patience, and attention, the tools and ingredients are mostly easier to acquire. In many cases, hard-to-find ingredients aren't required at all, but are an optional bonus to your practice.

Each of the following methods works by breaking down letters and symbols into their basic components. Doing this creates a transition from the language of the conscious mind to the imagery of the subconscious. As you experiment with each approach, remember that the infusion of your energy into the creation of the sigil is more important than which method you use or how good it looks when it's complete. Find a technique that you can connect with, because that *connection* is part of what makes a sigil so potent, not the approach itself. You'll know that it feels right when you find satisfaction or joy in its creation.

Method 1: Make a Sigil from Letters

By transforming letters into an image, you'll be shifting the language of your intention into a symbol that speaks more loudly to your subconscious and the universe.

1. Write your intention statement across the top of a clean sheet of paper. Try all capital letters to see if that gives the sigil more power and structure, if that feels right to you.

I AM PROTECTED

2. Next, cross out all the vowels.

I̸ A̸M PR̸O̸TE̸CTE̸D

3. Now cross out any repeating letters. You should be left with a series of consonants that will make up the structure of your sigil.

I̸ A̸M PR̸O̸TE̸CTE̸D

4. Write them out separately below your statement.

MPRTCD

5. Starting with the first of the letters that remains, draw it in the space underneath your statement. You'll see three options below, reflecting a range of styles to hopefully inspire your own:

A.   B.   C.

6. Mark off that letter, or put a dot under it, so you know that you have used it.

7. Now draw the next letter connecting to the first one, anywhere that it feels right to you. It can be sideways, upside down, backward, or at any angle you wish. You can even reuse the lines from one letter to form part of another one.

8. Repeat that process until all the letters you had not crossed out have been incorporated together into a single form.

9. From here, you can leave it the way it is, if it feels done to you, or you can redraw it as many times as you like, making the letters flow more or angle more. Add dots, circles, or lines if you like.

10. Once you feel it's done, redraw it on a clean sheet of paper to use when working your magic. You can cut away the excess paper or leave it the way it is.

Method 2: Make a Sigil from Shapes

You can also create effective sigils using shapes. These shapes can come from using the basic shapes of the letters in your intention statement. They can be symbols and shapes that have universal meaning. Or they can simply be forms that have personal meaning to you. Feel free to use any combination in a way that feels right to you.

1. Create your intention statement. Remember to keep it simple. Write it out however you like.

2. Cross out the vowels and duplicate letters.

3. Start figuring out which shapes you'd like to use.

   A. Find the shapes that make up each letter's basic components. Take the capital letter "L": it's composed of two straight lines, a long vertical one and a shorter horizontal one.

   M G R T F L

   B. If you are using symbolic shapes, find or create shapes that can represent the main words in your statement. You can get creative with this one, as long as the shapes represent that word to *you*. Examples might be: a starburst that represents "I am," or two wavy lines in a "V" shape representing hands that are cupped open.

4. Connect the letter shapes and/or symbol shapes in any way that you like, making sure not to leave out representation for any important words or energies from your intention.

A.   B.   OR   OR

5. Once you have your sigil, draw it again on a clean piece of paper to use in your sigil magic.

Method 3: Use a Sigil Created by Someone Else

If you really love the artistic style of someone else's sigils and can't seem to replicate it yourself, then you can ask that practitioner to create a sigil for you. You'll still have to take the time to create your own intention statement first, however.

In such cases, it's a good idea to complete an energetic exchange, meaning you give the other practitioner something in return for their work. This will help disconnect the original artist's energy from the sigil. Money works, but it could also be a service or item that you can barter with, if they're open to it.

As long as your intention statement is strong, the sigil you receive should work for you. What you should never do, however, is take a sigil from someone without their permission, or unless it is obviously given freely to the public domain. Doing so can be considered a copyright infringement, and the artist's energy may still be attached to it, which will affect your magic.

If your sigil artist is someone that you see in person on a regular basis, they can hand you a paper copy of the sigil, or if you find someone online, they will likely send you a digital version of the sigil. You will be in charge of activating your new sigil to finish making it yours alone.

BEGINNER-FRIENDLY SIGILS

Here are a few examples of simple, beginner-friendly sigils. You can see from these that sigil crafting can vary in style, method, and overall appearance.

Letter style, "I am full of confidence."

I AM FULL OF CONFIDENCE

I AM FULL ØF CØNFIDENCE

M F L C N D

There are three different free-form sigils below that use these letters. For each, you'll find both a straight-forward and a more-embellished approach. Can you pick out the individual letters? Notice that when creating "F" it also created an "L." By adding a line to the letter "C," (or a star in one case), a lowercase "d" formed. In many cases, other letters just show up.

Letter-shape style, "I am protected."

I AM PROTECTED

I AM PRØTECTED

MPRTCD

This style is a bit more structured than the previous one. By breaking down each of the remaining letters into their basic shapes, you can see that many of the shapes are the same or similar. In this case, include your repeated shapes so that each letter is represented in whole, even if the combined shapes no longer look like the original letter.

Shape-only style, "Abundance flows to me with ease."

ABUNDANCE FLOWS TO ME WITH EASE

This sigil includes an open chalice to represent abundance, a couple of flowing lines, and arrows to indicate direction. The opening in the circle represents the "ease," the flow penetrating any existing barriers. You can see here that you can make your sigil as simple or as ornate as you like.

Activating Your Sigil

Activation starts your magic, like the spark that lights the fire, at any time of your choosing. In some cases, you might want to time your activation with a moon phase, astrological position, day of the week, or special event like a holiday or birthday.

There are many methods to choose from, or you can come up with your own approach based on your intuition and preference. You can bury a sigil in the earth, cover it with crystals or herbs, blow on it, expose it to incense, trace it with essential oils, place it in the sunlight and let it fade, or place it in the light of a full moon. You can stare at one spot on the paper, off to the side of the sigil, until the sigil seems to disappear from your vision for a moment.

You may wish to use a method of activation that matches your sigil on an elemental level, such as burning your vitality sigil or submerging your intuition sigil in water. The more you learn about the correspondences of the planets, elements, crystals, colors, and other tools, the more options you'll have for pairing your sigil with an activation type that lends a little extra strength to the process.

Disposing of Your Sigil

It's important to dispose of a sigil respectfully once it's run its course. That could mean the energy has dissipated, your goals have changed, or it has already produced the result you were looking for. If you'd like to dispose of your sigil, but it feels as though it is still active, then first say something like "I now release any energy that remains in this sigil back to where it came from. This sigil is now null and void. Thank you."

After deactivation, you can tear your sigil in half. Then consider tearing it up into smaller pieces, to avoid anyone down the line seeing it and connecting to it accidentally. You can simply recycle a sigil drawn on paper. But be mindful of any other magical ingredients you have used that could affect the environment. Avoid littering, polluting water tables, or leaving things that can be dangerous to animals or children.

Reusing your sigil is also an option. In that case, after deactivating it, you could put it safely away in a trinket box or between the pages of a journal.

Now It's Your Turn

Now the good part: Putting what you've learned so far into practice.

If this is your first intention statement, ask yourself what your uppermost desire is right now. Try to get to the very core so that you're asking with clarity and specificity for what you truly want in this moment.

Use the space provided below to write it out.

Next, follow your intuition by picking the sigil-drawing method that feels right to you. Or let the theme of your intention help you choose, like using the letters method for a communication spell. Feel free to experiment with a few approaches. Just remember to hold your intention in your mind and maintain focus while crafting your sigil. It can help to repeat your intention over and over as you work, or to visualize the outcome as if it has already happened. Have fun and be true to yourself as you create.

Incorporating Sigil Magic Alongside Other Spell Work

Sigil magic, as described so far, constitutes a full and complete practice in its own right. But it can also be used to amplify the power behind any other spell work or rituals in which you participate. After all, it directly represents your spell's intention. It adds to the focus of the magic and makes it personal to you.

You could, for example, place a sigil next to, or underneath, a corresponding candle to incorporate your sigil magic into candle magic. The candle can even be the method you're using to activate your sigil. Each form of magic works in synergy to strengthen the other. Placing a protection sigil on your altar could be a way to protect your magic from outside influence. In this instance, you are using sigil magic to work *on* your other magic. Perhaps you are crafting a healing oil for yourself or a friend. Creating a healing sigil and placing it under the bottle of oil for a period of time will imbue that oil with the sigil's intention.

Here's where you get to use your imagination. As long as the intention of the sigil doesn't work against the spell's purpose, then you're good to go. For example, if you're performing prosperity candle magic, a sigil that has an intention to find emotional balance wouldn't relate well, but a matching prosperity sigil, or one for a promotion, would.

No matter what kind of additional magic you may decide to practice, sigil magic is a perfect complement to it.

KEEP A RECORD OF YOUR SIGIL WORK

Keeping records of your magical workings in a journal will allow you to keep track of which spells worked, which didn't, and likely why they didn't. You might then be able to tinker with and develop your magic further. Revisiting your spells could also help clarify your desires as time goes on.

If your notes are to be used to improve your results, include the following information:

- Date, day of the week, time of day, moon phase and placement, and current weather. Rain can actually have an effect on magic, adding the water element to anything you do.

- Your intention statements

- The method used to create your sigil

- A copy of your sigil

- Where, when, and how you activated your sigil

- What, if any, other magic was used in conjunction with your sigil magic

- How long you plan to wait for results

- A blank space to write your results at a later time

Harness Your Magic Wherever You Go

Sigil magic can enhance your life in many ways, and once you get the hang of it, you'll be able to access your magic anywhere.

By continuing your sigil practice, you'll find that you become clear on what it is you really want out of life, because you'll be crafting and simplifying your desires into intention statements. Additionally, by keeping records of your progress, you will learn more about yourself, how your magic manifests itself, and better ways to incorporate it into your daily life.

In clarifying your desires and sending them out to the universe in symbolic language via your sigils, you are also telling your subconscious to receive that manifestation, whether it's a change in point of view, lifestyle, environment, or circumstance. Your subconscious and the universe speak the same language, after all.

So, whether you're a "baby witch" or have had many years of experience, you can begin to access the magic of sigils as soon as you craft one. You can start exploring and expanding your practice now with just a clear mind, a pen, and some paper.

This next chapter will enhance your understanding and practice of sigil magic even more with many tips and tricks, including ways to cleanse yourself and your ritual space, incorporate the natural world into your sigil magic, and use magical ingredients to augment your sigil work.

CHAPTER 3

Prepare Yourself for Practicing Sigil Magic

Preparing your mind, your body, and the space around you is an important first step in casting many spells and rituals. In some cases, it's written into the spell itself, because the time, attention, and *intention* that go into physical and mental preparation help you begin to focus your energy toward your desired goal.

In this chapter, you'll explore many different aspects of preparation, the unique purposes each serve across magical traditions, and the ways you might choose to incorporate them into your own practice.

You'll also discover how the natural world can be an active participant in your sigil creation and spell work. For example, the phases of the moon, time of day, and even weather can have an effect on your magic.

The chapter also delves into many of the components, ingredients, and tools used in magic. Just remember that the priority is to use what works for you and your lifestyle. Implementing the different materials and alternative magical practices should happen at your own pace, when you feel comfortable. No matter the physical space or the resources available, sigil magic can be performed with as little as moving your finger through the air. If the energy and intention are there, magic will find a way.

Your Space Should Support Your Magic Work

Preparation typically begins with the creation of what some would call a "sacred space," a place typically in your home or in nature where you feel secure, empowered, and free from distractions. Think of your sacred space as an environment you rebuild for yourself each time you use it. It should fit right in with your magical practice and your lifestyle. It could be a kitchen table, a desk area in an office or bedroom, or the coffee table in your living room. Even an empty shelf or a windowsill can be used. Just be sure to pick a place and a time where the magic you craft will not get disturbed by anyone while it's running its course. It also doesn't have to be a *permanent* room or area dedicated only to magic. You can prepare an area, practice your magic, and, once it's complete, clean up the magical tools and go back to your daily routine.

The following details will describe the process of turning a regular area of your home into a sacred space for practicing sigil magic.

GET RID OF CLUTTER

Once you have chosen the place where you would like to practice your sigil magic, take a look around and see if you have any clutter that can be tidied up.

Clearing out unnecessary items creates a physical, mental, and spiritual opening that will allow you to focus on the task at hand and practice your magic free from distraction. Even if the clutter itself isn't distracting, there could also be some stagnant energy built up in the belongings themselves.

So, either remove the items or straighten and reorganize them. This way, any visual chaos that clutter might cause won't break your focus as you're performing your spells, and any heavy energy will have been released by moving items around. This will help bring in a new flow of magical energy to fulfill your goals.

CLEAN AND CLEANSE

Physical and energetic cleaning and cleansing allow you to clear out as much old energy as possible, making way for the magic that fulfills your new desires.

Physically cleanse the space first using whatever it is you generally clean with.

Then it's time to cleanse the energy. There are many tools and methods that work well for this, including incense or room spray. In this practice, you pass each item through the smoke or spray to purify it. If what you're using produces smoke, be aware of your smoke detectors, and open at least one window to let the smoke out.

Another approach is to mix sea salt and water, bless the mixture, asking the ingredients to work together for the purpose of cleansing, and sprinkle it around the room in a counterclockwise direction. You can also try holding your dominant hand over the tools and speaking something like the following incantation, as you imagine anything unconstructive leaving the object: "I command all negativity to depart from this object immediately, and invoke upon it the highest readiness and good to fulfill the purpose I have in mind. Thank you."

Please be sure that whatever you choose—and it is up to you—is procured and used in a respectful manner. You'll know you're done when you feel a sense of lightness or a brightness that wasn't present before you started.

REMOVE DISTRACTIONS

Distractions and interruptions are sometimes unavoidable, but, if possible, make sure that you have minimized the possibility of being disturbed in the middle of a spell.

Try to choose a time when you think you'll be left alone by other people who may live with you or who may visit, and when any pets are blissfully sleeping or preoccupied with their own adventures. Turn the ringer off on your phone if that's feasible, and power down any other devices. If there is an outside noise that's distracting, like a neighbor or construction, perhaps a fan or white noise machine could help tone it down.

If you are interrupted anyway, don't worry; you can pick up right where you left off. Take a deep breath, read your intention again, and get back into the right frame of mind for your magic. Preparing doesn't mean that you'll always have complete control of your space; just do what you can and adapt.

GATHER EVERYTHING YOU NEED

The gathering process can be its own ritual of sorts, one that imbues the items you'll use with energy that matches your spell work and that centers and grounds your mind. Unless it's a magical emergency, try not to rush and grab at the last moment.

Make a list of everything that you'll need, even if you think it's already stored in your work space. This will help make sure you not only have everything with you once you begin your magic, but that you have consciously connected with each item.

Even if something seems obvious, like paper, a pen, a lighter, or an intention statement you've written out in advance, include them on your list to give them their due attention. Be present while you're collecting your tools and ingredients so you can treat each with respect and gratitude.

Let the Natural World In

The magical world is entwined with the natural one. In order for you to connect with magic, you will need to connect to nature as well. You can do this by making sure that the energy coming from your intention, yourself, and your environment are all aligned.

One aspect of alignment is *timing*. Depending on the traditions that resonate with you, this could include the current phase of the moon and what zodiac sign it's in, equinox and solstice dates, and the hour of sunrise or sunset. By being aware of nature's cycles and the different kinds of energy each provides, you'll be able to make sure your spells are supported by the world around you.

Another aspect of environmental alignment is *elemental*. The four natural elements—earth, air, fire, and water—and their associations have an effect on your magic.

The more that you learn about and use these corresponding natural energies, the more you'll be aware of them in your everyday life as well.

THE SEASONS

Spring, summer, autumn, and winter all have different basic energies associated with them. Even in parts of the world where the weather doesn't change much during the year, there are still established start dates for the seasons. The equinoxes mark when day and night are of equal length, the summer solstice is the longest day of the year, and the winter solstice is the shortest. These dates are usually marked in calendars and are opposite for northern and southern hemispheres.

Below are the seasons listed with their magical and everyday associations:

SPRING EQUINOX: is correlated with birth, growth, anything new, the element of air, and the direction East. Knowing the direction allows you to face that way while doing a particular spell, to better align with it.

SUMMER SOLSTICE: relates to passion, action, vitality, the element of fire, and the direction South

AUTUMN EQUINOX: is connected with emotions, dreams, intuition, the element of water, and the direction West

WINTER SOLSTICE: is associated with healing, being at rest, the element of earth, and the direction North

THE PHASES OF THE MOON

Each of the eight phases of the moon has its own influence over magic as well. You can find the current lunar phase on some print calendars, or confirm it online.

The phases and how they are aligned with magic are listed here in order of their appearance in the sky.

NEW MOON: cleansing, unlimited possibility, planning your future

WAXING CRESCENT: setting intentions, new beginnings, focusing on the details

FIRST QUARTER: taking action, gaining momentum, attracting things to you

WAXING GIBBOUS: pausing and observing

FULL MOON: peak energy, charging magical tools, enhancing intuition

WANING GIBBOUS: resting and recharging, any spell that removes negativity, protection spells

THIRD QUARTER: receiving, releasing, giving back

WANING CRESCENT: relaxing, showing gratitude

As the moon grows, you may benefit from practicing sigil magic that brings things to you. As it wanes, you may prefer to perform magic that releases or goes within to give insight.

THE POSITION OF THE SUN

The strength of the light given off by the sun varies according to your location, the time of year, and the weather. This intensity of light can influence the energy of your magic.

Choose a time of the day to activate a specific intention using the general guidelines below. "Solar noon" refers to the actual peak of the sun in the sky at your location in the world, which is almost never exactly 12:00 p.m.; you can look it up online to find the time.

SUNRISE TO SOLAR NOON: any magic that is intended to increase something in your life such as abundance, health, or to bring in something new

JUST AFTER SOLAR NOON TO SUNSET: magic that is intended to take something out of your life, such as negativity or old habits that no longer serve you

SUNSET TO SUNRISE: magic that is related to revealing secrets, or anything that may be hidden from you

THE ELEMENTS

The basic alchemical elements of earth, air, fire, and water can play a large role in your magical practice and lifestyle as well. You'll discover that these elements have an association with almost everything, including herbs, food, magical tools, seasons, the weather, colors, and planets.

Certain energies are associated with each of the four elements, which can help you orient your sigil magic.

EARTH: grounding, dark, cold, solidity, foundations, resources, protection, nurturing, birth and rebirth, resting, restoration, tranquility, patience, the physical body, Venus, and Saturn

AIR: flowing, lightness, harmony, communication, contracts, justice, legal matters, pen and paper, the mind, travel, Mercury, Jupiter, and Uranus

FIRE: action, speed, heat, passion, vitality, conflict, sports and exercise, Mars, Pluto, and the sun

WATER: adaptability, conformity, compassion, empathy, intuition, emotions, receptivity, the moon, and Neptune

PLANETARY MOVEMENTS

You can use planetary influences in your magic. There are two key guidelines to be aware of when casting spells: where a planet is located currently in the zodiac, and whether or not it's in retrograde motion.

By looking up which planet corresponds with your intention, then finding the zodiac sign it's traveling through, you'll know if that planet's impact is currently weakened or strengthened. The stronger a planet's influence, the more you will be able to use ite in your spell directly. If it's weak, then you can augment it by using other ingredients that correspond to your sigil.

The term "retrograde" means that a planet appears to be moving backward in the sky. When that's the case, only perform spells that match that inward-moving energy, such as those that change the way you feel about or perceive something, or those meant to be protective.

Think of the planets as allies in your practice.

DAYS OF THE WEEK

The days of the week were originally named after deities but were later associated with the energies of the seven planets known at that time.

Find a fitting day of the week to practice different types of magic based on the ruling planet for that day.

MONDAY (THE MOON): emotion, intuition, cycles of all kinds, and the element of water

TUESDAY (MARS): action, passion, conflict, and the fire element

WEDNESDAY (MERCURY): the mind, communication, short-distance travel, elementary education, contracts, and the element of air

THURSDAY (JUPITER): luck, expansion, legal matters, organized religion, higher education, far-reaching goals, long-distance travel, and air or fire elements

FRIDAY (VENUS): beauty, love, financial matters, values, art, and the earth and water elements

SATURDAY (SATURN): authority figures, time, boundaries, limitations, rules, and the earth element

SUNDAY (THE SUN): health, vitality, growth, wealth, and the element of fire

LEAVE DISRESPECT AT THE DOOR

Respect is a fundamental part of magic, and it means keeping an open mind when learning about traditions that are different than your own. It also means honoring boundaries so as not to appropriate rituals that are sacred to other cultures. Appropriating rituals puts at risk the very understanding of a ritual's cultural origins, values, and historical context.

As a magic user, it's both a calling and a responsibility to bring respect for other cultures into your craft. The use of certain ritual practices and ingredients is considered cultural appropriation if practiced by those who do not identify as part of that culture.

By learning more about a culture's history, you'll be able to determine whether or not something you're intending to incorporate into your magical practice is cultural appropriation, why it's considered so, and how to use possible alternatives. In cases when you are able to incorporate a ritual or tradition from another culture into your own practice without appropriation, it's crucial to treat the magic, tools, and ingredients being shared with the veneration and attribution they deserve.

In taking proactive steps to respect all cultures and magical traditions, you can direct the energy of your sigil magic away from unintentional harm. And researching the origins of an ingredient or practice, and whether its use is considered disrespectful to the culture that it belongs to, can open your mind to new viewpoints as well.

Magical Ingredients to Have on Hand

The reason behind many ingredients and tools used in magic is to draw you into the right mindset. Smells, sounds, and colors can all evoke unique associations, emotions, and memories. Spells will call for different ingredients based on the energy they require. Nevertheless, while spells may call for specific ingredients, you have the freedom to make substitutions based on what is available to you and what most inspires you.

It's important that every part of a spell, down to the tools that you use, aligns with your values. So, try to be mindful of where and how your ingredients are sourced. This could mean looking for items that are made or grown locally, or those harvested in a sustainable manner. Or it could mean refraining from using synthesized chemicals or scents. As with your rituals overall, it's your responsibility to make sure the ingredients you use do not cross the boundaries of cultural appropriation.

Next you'll find the names and magical properties of some of the ingredients you may want to gather and keep on hand. But the bottom line is that you need to enter into any ritual with a mindset that aligns with your intention and your sigil. And showing your care and respect for your tools will make them more accessible to your magic.

ESSENTIAL OILS

Essential oils are distilled or extracted from plant material and are more portable and concentrated than the substances they were made from. These oils are widely used across many forms of magic because they all correspond to certain aspects of being human and can enhance the connection to a desired energy. You can anoint candles and other magical tools, apply them directly to your sigils, bathe with a few drops in your water, or even use them on your skin after testing for sensitivity and allergies. None of these oils should be ingested.

Oils can be used alone or together, and you can even create your own purpose oils like a "Banishing Oil," using combinations of essential oils and herbs.

Here are a few common magical themes and their corresponding essential oils.

ABUNDANCE, PROSPERITY: almond, coconut, spearmint

CLEANSING: basil, hyssop, rosemary

COURAGE: angelica, borage, rose geranium, thyme

HEALTH: geranium, juniper, sunflower

LOVE: apple, avocado, cardamom, gardenia

MENTAL CLARITY: lavender, mustard, walnut

PROTECTION: acacia, bay, betony, carnation

HERBS, TEA LEAVES, AND SPICES

Use herbs, teas, and spices in your sigil magic to enhance the energies and outcomes of your intention statements.

You can burn them, eat or drink the ones that are safe to ingest, or sprinkle them on a sigil or around a candle. They make a great substitute for essential oils because they are often easier to obtain and more affordable.

You can use the list of essential oils to also determine herbs that you might find useful. Spices and teas can be great enhancements as well. Nutmeg, for example, boosts sigil magic that pertains to prosperity, luck, and health. Black pepper is excellent for protection and keeping secrets. Teas can be used in preparation by drinking them just before you start a ritual. Black, white, and green teas are used for strength and courage. Chamomile is wonderful for purification.

CANDLES

Candles add the element of fire to your ritual magic and are a common way to activate sigils. Be mindful of scented candles for your spell craft, as they may introduce new ingredients into your practice. For example, some candles are scented using natural essential oils, so you'd want to make sure the oil matches the intention of your spell.

If you do choose to use candles to enhance your sigil magic, there are several aspects to consider: wax type, wick type, and burn time. Any awareness you can bring regarding differences in sustainability and clean burning can only enhance your practice.

Learning color correspondences can enhance your sigil magic as well by lending the energy of a color wax to your intention. You can also use white as a substitute for any color.

In all your researching, remember that what matters most is to choose what works for you.

INCENSE

Burning incense is a time-honored practice in ceremony, ritual, and the practice of magic. When you use it in sigil magic, you are connecting to this tradition through the elements of air and fire. The scent will also help you align with your sigil's intention.

When purchasing incense, look for sustainability and avoid cultural appropriation. Instead of sage, for example, you can burn pine or cedar to chase away negative energies in your home, and instead of palo santo, which is sensitive to overharvesting, you might try a mix of frankincense and myrrh.

You can burn incense sticks, or resins and powders. For the latter, you will need a small fire-safe bowl or dish with sand in it and charcoal disks made especially for burning resins and powders. It can help to look for charcoal that is quick-lighting. For most spaces, you won't need the whole disk. It's perfectly fine to break them in halves or quarters.

CRYSTALS AND GEMS

Gemstones and crystals are wonderful complements to your sigil magic because they all have their own energetic properties that can enhance your spells. One way to use them is to place them on, or next to, your sigil while it's being activated, and then carry that stone with you as a way to keep your intention with you wherever you go.

Following are some common magical themes with their corresponding crystals and gemstones.

ABUNDANCE, PROSPERITY: aventurine, citrine, pyrite

CLEANSING: clear quartz, selenite, Shungite

COURAGE: bloodstone, carnelian, ruby

HEALTH: citrine, lapis lazuli, turquoise

LOVE: garnet, pink kunzite, rose quartz

MENTAL CLARITY: amazonite, amethyst, malachite

PROTECTION: black tourmaline, hematite, obsidian

Keep in mind that some stones, such as selenite, malachite, amethyst, and citrine, can be damaged by long exposure to water or sunlight.

CHARMS

The word "charm" can refer either to an incantation or to an object imbued with a magical intention thematically matching its shape. This latter interpretation is more commonly used today. The idea is that the object embodies its meaning by virtue of its form, like a key charm for "opening doors of opportunity" or a heart for love. You'll also frequently see coin charms used to represent abundance or prosperity, trees for growth or health, and lions for courage or leadership.

You could even come up with your own magical charms by asking yourself what a specific shape means to you. Or redefine an existing charm such as the key, for example. If it means something different to you, use it that way instead.

By using a charm that aligns with your intention statement, you can take your magic with you, or even wear it as a talisman if you like, without exposing your actual sigil.

DEITIES

Gods and goddesses can be found in a large variety of cultural pantheons and are often associated with, or considered watchers of, distinct aspects of the human experience. If it feels right to you, a deity can be called upon to enhance your sigil magic.

You could evoke the presence of a particular god or goddess to assist in your endeavors by creating a sigil using their name. Or perhaps they already have a sigil that was dedicated to them long ago. Ancient sigils are considered to be particularly powerful, having been charged with the energy of many people over generations. These sigils are different from the ones created today by individuals to represent their intention statements.

You can also use a symbolic representation to ask that a deity look over a spell, or your practice in general. For example, a small statuette of a cat might represent the Egyptian goddess Bastet, or a painting of Artemis might call the attention of the Greek goddess of the hunt.

SPECIAL PENS AND PAPERS

Another way to connect to your sigil magic in a profound way is through your tactile senses, using special papers or pens. Parchment paper, for example, has a certain look and feel that may evoke the past, and a calligraphy pen may carry a certain grace or significance in its use. There are also purpose inks such as Dragon's Blood and Money Drawing that you can make yourself for use with calligraphy pens. These inks are infused with herbs or resins that enhance their intention and, in turn, yours.

You could even use colored paper or ink for certain types of sigils, such as green or gold for money and abundance or red or pink for love. Any kind of paper or writing instrument that feels special to you can help you concentrate on your intention and enhance your magic. Using special pens and papers is absolutely optional.

A JOURNAL OR GRIMOIRE

Creating or acquiring a dedicated journal or grimoire is useful for this practice so that your notes are all in one place. You need to be able to go back and see what worked and what didn't, improving your magic.

You might look for a journal that meets your style and aesthetic. Perhaps one journal feels better in your hand than another, or is adorned with symbols or colors that attract you. Another consideration is whether you prefer blank pages, which are great for pasting or drawing images, or lined pages, which work better for lists and paragraphs.

Most important, choose a journal that *you* will enjoy writing in. It can be as plain or as fancy as you like. And while it should be treated as a special object, that doesn't mean you should be discouraged if you make a mistake; just correct it in any way that works for you and keep writing.

ITEMS FROM YOUR "BACKYARD"

With magic, you can treat the whole planet as your backyard. Just make sure that when you're collecting items, they don't belong to someone else, they aren't endangered, and you aren't causing harm.

You can collect seashells or river water, for example, to enhance water-related spells. Naturally discarded feathers work for air, rocks or dirt for earth, and lava stone or volcanic glass for fire. Fallen branches make great wands, if you choose to use one, and found coins are wonderful for money and abundance spells.

By bringing a magical awareness to your environment while living your everyday life, you'll begin to notice all kinds of items turning up for you. Just remember to cleanse them both physically and spiritually, and to give thanks before using them.

QUICK TIPS AND TOOLS

Here are some additional insights that might help you as you begin your sigil practice.

(0) To burn candles in your home safely, you can create temporary altar spaces out of a bathroom or kitchen sink, a fireplace if you have one, or even a stovetop.

(0) Incense smoke can be an irritant for some people and can set off sensitive smoke alarms in your home. As an alternative, you could mix distilled water and whichever herb you were planning on burning into a spray bottle.

(0) Always cleanse your tools and ingredients both physically and energetically (see Clean and Cleanse, page 32).

(0) Keep your magic secret. When you tell people about your active rituals, their awareness can automatically link them to the spells, influencing the energy and perhaps diverting the magic unintentionally. This could cause your spells to dissipate.

Practical Sigil Magic Is at Your Fingertips

Practical sigil magic is accessible to *anyone* who has an interest in living a magical lifestyle. It's a simple tool that effectively produces results when used correctly and with enough intent and focus. Sigils are a versatile way of communicating your desires to your own subconscious and to the universe. Because of their adaptability, you can use them in ways that connect and align with your core being, while also fitting into your current daily routines.

You have now journeyed through some of the fundamentals of the magical world, including the origins of sigils and magic, the importance of focus and mindset, setting up your magical work space, effectively creating your intention statements, and, of course, viewing several ways to craft your sigils. You have also been introduced to the whats and whys of the basic tools and ingredients you can use, ways to record your magical progress in a manner that works for you, methods for incorporating sigil magic with other forms of magic, and ways you might enhance your craft with nature's cycles.

Now you are ready to take action and turn the theory into practice. Part 2 of this book will have you applying sigil magic to your life in areas ranging from self-empowerment to relationship growth.

PART II

UNLEASH YOUR SIGIL MAGIC

This part of the book is where the magic happens; now is the time that you get to practice your craft. While all the spells that follow include sigils, each one also draws inspiration from different rituals, visualizations, meditations, and remedies. These variations and enhancements will allow you to get a feel for what might work best for you and your lifestyle.

This part of the book is organized into categories such as self-care, general health and well-being, relationships, inspiration and abundance, connection to the natural world, and nourishing your home. You'll discover spells to find love, clear up miscommunication, or bring joy when it's challenging to do so. You can bond with nature through solstice and equinox rituals, and even help mitigate the unwanted effects of Mercury retrograde. You'll practice magic that can assist you in finding gratitude, setting compassionate boundaries, and letting go of those things in life that no longer serve you.

Each spell has a specific intended purpose, lists materials, and identifies any useful timing guidelines, such as an ideal phase of the moon or time of day, and elements to which the spell may be attuned. Here are some guidelines that apply to all the spells to follow:

◎ When a spell mentions cleansing and purifying your ritual space and tools but does not offer specific instructions, you can always use incense or room spray. But it's open to you to clear the energy however you feel works best. See Clean and Cleanse, page 32, for more detailed options. All the spells in this book list cleansing as the first step, assuming that you will create the sigil and cast the spell in one sitting. But it is okay if you want to create the intention and sigil one day and then later—hours, days, weeks, even months—activate it or perform the spell. In that situation, cleanse the space, tools, and ingredients prior to activation, not prior to sigil making.

◎ Make sure always to keep a cup of water nearby when using fire in your spells. If a ritual requires you to burn a candle all the way down, it can be treated as a passive part of the spell. You can take your eyes off the candle so long as you practice safety. Make sure that you extinguish it if you are leaving your home while it is still burning, and relight it when you return.

◎ Some of the rituals require you to make a final copy of the sigil onto colored paper. Other rituals make this step optional, and still other rituals do not mention making a final copy at all. Unless it is a required step in the spell, making a second, clean copy of the sigil is up to you. Just make sure that the sigil you use doesn't have erasures and corrections; it should be clear and without distractions.

- If a spell does not otherwise specify a way to dispose of a sigil—or that you should keep it—always dispose of ingredients in a respectful manner with gratitude.

- While the spells may recommend crystals, incense, and oils as enhancements, keep in mind that every spell can be distilled down to just intention, sigil creation, activation, and disposal. The rest is up to you, your lifestyle, and your magical intuition.

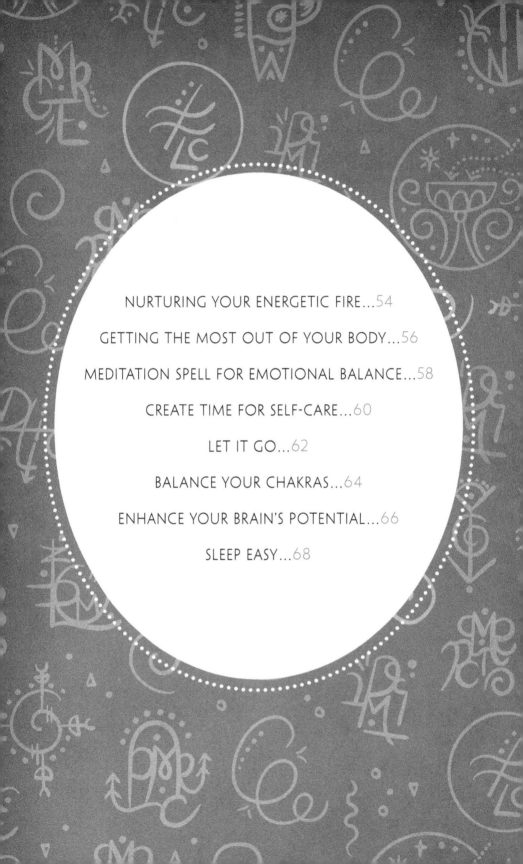

CHAPTER 4

Tend to Your Mind, Body, and Spirit

The magic in this chapter is geared toward self-care for your mind, body, and spirit. This can involve many different things, including rest and relaxation, general wellness, body movement, mental balance, spiritual balance, or even just taking time for yourself. It's not necessary to sacrifice your health or well-being to please others or accomplish goals, so a little nudge toward balancing your needs with life's demands and the needs of others is helpful. For those who already have a handle on balancing their health with other stressors, there are a couple of spells that offer peak enhancement.

While these spells are not meant to take the place of a health professional's advice, they can be used in conjunction with whatever kind of care you might be receiving. Any of the following sigils and accompanying spells can be tailored so that they are unique to you and your desires. They can be your aid to a more balanced and productive life.

NURTURING YOUR ENERGETIC FIRE

PURPOSE: To increase or spark your inner vim and vigor. This spell can give you physical and mental energy either when you are generally feeling worn down, or when you know you'll specifically need a little extra fire, like before running a marathon.

SETTING: Your ritual space at any time, but it will be most effective just after sunrise on a Sunday or Tuesday to capture the energy of the sun or Mars

CASTING TIME: 30 minutes

PRIMARY INGREDIENTS:

Incense, burner, and lighter/matches, or other purification tools

Pen/pencil and paper

Red, yellow, or orange paper or ink, for copying the sigil

Fire-safe bowl, cup, or vessel, with sand filling it about halfway

ADDITIONS OR SUBSTITUTIONS:

Lava stone or carnelian gemstone

"Sun" purpose oil, essential oils of sweet orange or lemon, or an actual orange or lemon

1. Cleanse your space and energetically purify your tools and ingredients, one at a time, with incense or another chosen method.

2. Write your intention statement. It should be something that states your increase of energy as a present fact. It could even be about how your life might be different with more energy such as "I have enough energy to . . ."

3. Craft your sigil using the method that feels right to you, using letters, shapes, symbols, and/or other sigils for inspiration. If you like, you can refer back to the guidance under "There Are a Variety of Methods for Creating Sigils," beginning on page 19.

4. Copy your sigil onto the colored paper.

5. Place your sigil in your fire-safe vessel while staring at it and envisioning what it might feel like to have your intention fulfilled.

6. If you have chosen to use the lava stone or carnelian and oil, you may anoint the stone with any of the oils, or rub the rind from the actual fruit on it. Then place the stone between you and the fire-safe vessel, touching it if possible.

7. Set the sigil on fire, and wait for it to finish burning. As it burns, continue to envision the outcome of your intention statement, and conjure up the feelings you might have when that intention gets fulfilled.

8. If you used a stone, make sure it's *completely cooled* before touching it, and carry it with you in any way you like. If your stone feels as though it could use a recharge, you can repeat this ritual using the same sigil design.

GETTING THE MOST OUT OF YOUR BODY

PURPOSE: This is a long-term spell intended to enhance your body's ability to perform and enjoy physical activity. This is not a heal-all; it's about making the best of what you already have while respecting any physical limitations.

SETTING: Your ritual space at any time, but most effective on a Sunday, which represents joy and vitality, or during a full moon, which provides enhanced power to any spell

CASTING TIME: 30 minutes

PRIMARY INGREDIENTS:

Incense, burner, lighter/matches, or other purification tools

Pen/pencil and paper

Bowl or pot, filled with soil or dirt

ADDITIONS OR SUBSTITUTIONS:

Potted plant that you love instead of an empty pot with soil, or you can perform this spell outside, wherever there is dirt that you can dig into and where no one would accidentally disturb a buried sigil

Something that will protect your floor or altar space from the soil or dirt

Green paper or pen, to copy sigil

Moss agate or tree agate gemstone

1. Cleanse your space and energetically purify your tools and ingredients, one at a time, with incense or another chosen method.

2. Write your intention statement. It could be something about your body working at its maximum capacity, achieving more balance and coordination, or even finding full enjoyment in a particular physical activity.

3. Design your sigil while envisioning yourself performing at your physical best. Then, if you choose to use it, copy your image onto the green paper.

4. Lay down the item you've chosen to protect your space from dirt.

5. Staring at your sigil, envision your energy being grounded into the earth, all the way to the core of the planet.

6. While holding that vision, bury your sigil facedown in the pot or in the dirt.

7. If you're using a gemstone, bury it with your sigil. Just remember where it is, because you will dig up the gemstone in twenty-four hours so you can carry it with you. The sigil will remain buried.

8. Place the bowl or pot in a safe place near a window, if possible, and where it won't be disturbed. Leave your sigil buried for as long as you feel it's working.

MEDITATION SPELL FOR EMOTIONAL BALANCE

....

PURPOSE: This meditation can help you find balance in your emotions so you can move through them with ease. Use it whenever you feel out of sorts or in need of a space to reflect on how you feel.

SETTING: A comfortable sitting position where you can stay for 15 to 20 minutes. The best time is just before going to bed or before a nap and on a Monday, which is ruled by the moon and the water element.

CASTING TIME: 30 minutes

....

PRIMARY INGREDIENTS:
Incense, burner, and lighter/matches, or other purification tools

Pen/pencil and paper

Glass of drinking water

ADDITIONS OR SUBSTITUTIONS:
Blue paper or pen, for copying the sigil

Moonstone or azurite gemstone

1. Cleanse your space and energetically purify your tools, one at a time, with incense or another chosen method.

2. Write an intention that brings in balance rather than negates any emotion you might be feeling. The purpose is not to invalidate feelings, but rather something like "I move through my difficult emotions in a healthy manner."

3. Create a sigil using any method you'd like. Inspire yourself with a calming, balancing vison as you draw, such as a field of flowers or a placid body of water.

4. Copy your sigil onto the colored paper or using your colored pen, if using.

5. Take your sigil, hold it to your chest near your heart, and envision what your life looks like when you are emotionally balanced. Now, sitting comfortably, close your eyes, relax, and take several deep, long breaths.

6. Breathe and relax each muscle while repeating your intention statement in your mind. Keep your sigil on your chest in a way that is comfortable. Remain this way for 15 to 20 minutes. If a physical sensation intrudes on your awareness, feel free to adjust. Then turn your focus back to your breathing and your intention statement.

7. When you're done with the meditation, place your sigil faceup under the glass of water. If you're using a gemstone, place it next to, and touching, the glass of water.

8. Go to sleep. As soon as you wake up, drink the glass of water and dispose of your sigil in a respectful manner. If you used a gemstone, carry it with you as you like.

CREATE TIME FOR SELF-CARE

PURPOSE: This spell can help you create time for self-care—and also works when you feel overwhelmed or just need a break—without feeling like you are abandoning any of your responsibilities. It does this by tapping into the planetary energy of Saturn, which rules time, boundaries, and authority.

SETTING: Your ritual space, most effective on a Saturday morning

CASTING TIME: 20 minutes

PRIMARY INGREDIENTS:
Incense, burner, and lighter/matches, or other purification tools

Pen/pencil and paper

Graphite pencil, for circling sigil

Eraser

Glass jar, filled halfway with dirt or soil

ADDITIONS OR SUBSTITUTIONS:
Rose quartz crystal

1. Cleanse your space and energetically purify your tools, one at a time, with incense or another chosen method.

2. Write down your intention statement emphasizing your desire to incorporate more time for self-care into your life. It's not about taking anything away.

3. Draw your sigil to reflect what self-care looks like to you. It can be anything that makes you feel whole and in balance.

4. When the sigil is complete, use the graphite pencil, which is associated with Saturn, and in a clockwise direction, draw a complete circle around your sigil—even if you've already incorporated a circle into your original design. This new circle represents restriction or *not* having enough time to fulfill your intention.

5. As you visualize practicing self-care on a regular basis, erase that same circle in a counterclockwise direction. Once the circle is erased, take your sigil and place it in the jar on top of the dirt. Do not bury it, but rather allow it to be touching the earth and air elements simultaneously. Place the crystal on top of the sigil, if using.

6. Set the jar in a safe place where it will not be disturbed, preferably in the dark, until you feel that this intention has been fulfilled.

ꞈLET IT GO

PURPOSE: If you feel that you're having trouble letting go of an event, memory, or emotion, use this spell for an energetic release. Do not run this spell on a person, only the emotion you associate with that person. There are spells in chapter 6 for safely setting boundaries with others.

SETTING: Your ritual space at any time, but most effective during the third quarter moon phase, or on a Monday between solar noon and sunset

CASTING TIME: 10 minutes to perform the first part of the ritual, plus 10 minutes 24 hours later

PRIMARY INGREDIENTS:
Incense, burner, and lighter/matches, or other purification tools

Pen/pencil and paper

Feather of any color, from any bird, as long as the bird wasn't harmed in the giving of its feather. You will be discarding this feather as part of the process, so make sure it is not a treasured keepsake.

Dry, clean glass

ADDITIONS OR SUBSTITUTIONS:
Sky-blue paper or pen

1. Cleanse your space and energetically purify your tools, one at a time, with incense or another chosen method.

2. Craft and write down an intention statement that concentrates on releasing that which no longer serves you.

3. Draw the sigil using the method of your choice, feeling what it might be like to be free from the attachment to this emotion, object, or situation. Make a copy of your sigil on the colored paper, if you wish.

4. Place your sigil in front of you, and rest the feather on top. Set the glass upside down, over the feather and sigil.

5. While holding your dominant hand over the glass, speak your intention statement loudly. If you are in a space that cannot be disturbed by sound, call it out loudly in your mind.

6. Walk away, leaving the items there for now, and go about your day. Come back the next day, and remove the glass from the sigil. Pick up the feather, and release it to the wind, letting it take your attachments with it. Rip your sigil in half and discard it to mark the end of the spell.

BALANCE YOUR CHAKRAS

PURPOSE: You can achieve or enhance your general well-being by balancing all your energy centers, also known as chakras. There are seven main chakras in the body. On occasion, they can become imbalanced as a result of things like stress, poor eating habits, and too much or too little sleep, with too much energy flowing to some chakras in your body. When they are balanced, they support your organs and physical health.

SETTING: Your ritual space at any time, but most effective on any day or time representing the sun, such as Sunday

CASTING TIME: 15 minutes, plus time for the candle(s) to burn completely

PRIMARY INGREDIENTS:

Incense, burner, and lighter/matches, or other purification tools

Pen/pencil and paper

White candle

Candleholder

ADDITIONS OR SUBSTITUTIONS:

Instead of a white candle, use candles that match the colors of each chakra: red for the root, orange for the sacral, yellow for the solar plexus, green for the heart, blue for the throat, indigo for the third eye, and purple or violet for the crown.

Birthday candles can be an accessible option. If you use these, have a shallow fire-safe plate or bowl with sand in it to place the candles as you might on a cake.

There are also "chakra" candles available.

1. Cleanse your ritual space and energetically purify your tools and ingredients, one at a time, with incense or another chosen method.

2. Write down your intention that speaks about already having balanced chakras.

3. Create and draft your sigil while imagining swirling lights of color that match the chakras.

4. Place your sigil under the candleholder. If you have more than one candle, then place your sigil centrally in such a way that the candleholders all touch it, or create a copy of your sigil for each candle.

5. Take seven deep breaths, one for each chakra.

6. Light your candle(s) while saying your intention statement as many times as you like.

7. Let the candle(s) burn all the way down. If you need to leave home, extinguish the candle(s) and relight it (or them) when you return.

ENHANCE YOUR BRAIN'S POTENTIAL

PURPOSE: This is an effective spell for anything that requires mental focus, such as job performance, learning something new, or test-taking.

SETTING: Your ritual space at almost any time. This spell will be most effective on a Sunday, for the sun's energy, or a Wednesday, representing Mercury, intellect, and communication, between sunrise and solar noon. However, you should avoid Mercury retrograde unless you have nullified its effects first. You can use the spell Minimizing Mercury Retrograde (page 140) if you'd like.

CASTING TIME: 10 minutes, plus time for the candle to burn completely

PRIMARY INGREDIENTS:
Incense, burner, lighter/matches, or other purification tools

Candleholder

Orange candle

ADDITIONS OR SUBSTITUTIONS:
Orange paper or pen, to copy sigil

Dried or fresh rosemary

Mercury planetary oil or almond oil

A towel

1. Cleanse your space and energetically purify your tools and ingredients, one at a time, with incense or another chosen method.

2. Write down an intention statement that allows for the planetary power of Mercury to enhance your mental abilities.

3. When creating your sigil, imagine yourself as proficient in and performing with ease the mental tasks in which you are seeking improvement.

4. Copy your sigil onto the orange paper, if you're using this variation. Place the sigil under the candleholder.

5. If you choose, anoint the candle now with your oil by first dabbing some oil on your fingers. Starting at the top of the candle and working your way down, run the oil in a clockwise spiral. Place the candle in the holder.

6. If you choose to use rosemary, sprinkle it around the candleholder now in a clockwise direction.

7. Say your intention statement and light the candle while envisioning the results of this spell being fulfilled.

8. Let the candle burn all the way down. If you need to leave home, extinguish the candle, and relight it when you return.

SLEEP EASY

PURPOSE: For trouble sleeping, or when sleep doesn't seem as restful as usual. Water and the moon rule this spell as calming agents and meditation catalysts. If you have been diagnosed with insomnia, only use this spell in conjunction with your health professional's advice and treatment.

SETTING: Your sleeping area at any time, but most effective right before bedtime

CASTING TIME: 15 minutes to perform the spell, and 5 minutes when you next wake

PRIMARY INGREDIENTS:

Incense, burner, and lighter/matches, or other purification tools

Pen/pencil and paper

Glass or clear bowl of water so you can see your sigil through the bottom of it

Potted plant, or a plant in your yard that you can pour the water into

ADDITIONS OR SUBSTITUTIONS:

Blue food coloring

Moonstone

Agrimony, fresh, dried, or tincture

1. Cleanse your space and energetically purify your tools and ingredients, one at a time, with incense or another chosen method.

2. Write out your intention statement; it can be something like "I sleep easily and deeply."

3. Draw your sigil using any method of choice. Try to imagine what you will feel like when you've gotten a night of healing sleep and hold on to that as you create.

4. Place your sigil on a flat, safe surface that won't be disturbed. Place your glass or bowl of water on top of your sigil.

5. If you are using blue food coloring, add two drops to the water, then include the moonstone, and two pinches or drops of the agrimony.

6. Repeat your intention statement at least twice while staring down into your bowl of water at your sigil. Let your eyes lose their focus and relax. Remind yourself how great you feel when you've had enough restful sleep, and know that you will be getting that in just a few minutes.

7. Once you start feeling sleepy, go to bed.

8. When you wake up, pour the bowl of water, gemstone and all, into your chosen plant. Dispose of the sigil with respect.

CHAPTER 5

Strengthen Your Relationships with Friends, Family, and Lovers

All relationships are unique and, at times, any can become challenging to navigate. This chapter contains spells to help steer you through conflict, communication, and commitment. You'll also discover spells to assist you in romance, repairing, or even retreating from relationships. Keep in mind though that *none* of these spells are geared toward directly changing another person. Transforming the energy around a situation *between* yourself and another person, or changing your own energy, is a much more effective and ethical way to smooth out any discord and create new connections. Relationship spells do require a bit of attention and some forethought so that you can practice magic in ways that bring results without negatively impacting another person.

PEACEFUL RESOLUTION OF CONFLICT

PURPOSE: For untangling emotionally charged situations or restarting communication when you've seemingly reached a stalemate. Keep in mind that this spell brings in peace; it does not take away the original conflict.

SETTING: Your ritual space and a kitchen, if using the optional rose or rosemary water, at any time. This spell is most effective on a Friday, the day of the week ruled by Venus, a planet of the element water, which brings harmony to the situation.

CASTING TIME: 15 minutes, but if using the optional rose or rosemary water, allow 30 minutes to prepare that, and enough time to let it cool. This can be done ahead of time and stored in the refrigerator for up to a week.

PRIMARY INGREDIENTS:
Incense, burner, and lighter/matches, or other purification tools

Pen/pencil and paper

Sky-blue or light pink paper or pen

Glass of water, about three-quarters full

ADDITIONS OR SUBSTITUTIONS:
Rose or rosemary water instead of regular water, not for internal consumption

Amethyst or tiger's eye gemstone

1. Cleanse your space and energetically purify your tools and ingredients, one at a time, with incense or another chosen method.

2. If using the rose or rosemary water, take the petals of a rose or sprigs of rosemary and simmer them in a pot of water for about 5 minutes. Strain the plant matter out of the water, and let it cool to room temperature. Store it in an airtight container in the refrigerator until you are ready to use it

3. Write your intention statement. It could say something like "All is well and we are at peace with the outcome."

4. Draw your sigil using the symbol method or any approach that feels right to you. While doing so, picture how it might look once you achieve peace.

5. Copy your sigil onto your sky-blue or light pink paper or using your colored ink. Envision what it looks and feels like to have peaceful conflict resolution. Fold your sigil up so that it will fit into the glass of water or rose water, and place that paper in the glass. Don't worry if your paper floats; it's fine as long as it stays in the glass.

6. Place your glass in a safe place where it will not be disturbed until the water evaporates naturally over time. Discard the sigil with a mindset of respect and gratitude.

FINDING YOUR TRUE LOVE

PURPOSE: Use this spell to draw your true love into your life using the energy of the planet Venus. This spell requires that you trust your higher self and the universe to know more about who that person is than you do. If you bring in expectations or doubts about who you think you should love, you may inadvertently close yourself off to the magic of finding who you may love.

SETTING: It is most effective on a Friday between sunrise and solar noon, or during the new moon.

CASTING TIME: 15 minutes, plus time for the candle to burn completely

PRIMARY INGREDIENTS:
Rose incense, burner, and lighter/matches

Pen/pencil and paper

White candle

Candleholder

ADDITIONS OR SUBSTITUTIONS:
Light pink or green paper or pens, to copy sigil

Red or pink candle instead of white

Rose quartz or jade gemstone

1. Cleanse your space and energetically purify your tools and ingredients, one at a time, passing them through the smoke of the rose incense.

2. Decide on and write down an intention that keeps you open to love, however it comes to you. Consider something along the lines of "I am in a relationship with my true love."

3. Draw out your sigil. For inspiration, imagine the most amazing romantic relationship you've witnessed, in person or in fiction. Envision yourself in a relationship like that and how it feels to you.

4. Copy your sigil now on the pink or green paper, if using. Place your sigil under the candle in the candleholder. If using, place your gemstones next to and touching either the candleholder or sigil.

5. Speak your intention statement, trying not to visualize any specific person but to focus on the emotional core of loving and being loved.

6. Light the candle and say "thank you." Let the candle burn down completely. If you need to leave home, extinguish the candle, and relight it when you return.

7. Once the candle has burned down, carry with you the feelings that came up as you spoke your intention. If you used a gemstone, hold on to it as a reminder.

CLARITY OF COMMUNICATION

PURPOSE: To provide clarity where there has been a misunderstanding, or to prevent a miscommunication from occurring. This spell can help clear up the energy to uncover any cause of confusion in the communication process. Remember that this sigil should bring clarity in; it won't take back words of miscommunication that have already been spoken.

SETTING: Your ritual space at any time, but most effective on a Wednesday, the day ruled by Mercury, and facing east, if you'd like

CASTING TIME: 15 minutes, plus time for the candle to burn completely

PRIMARY INGREDIENTS:
Incense, burner, and lighter/matches, or other purification tools

Pen/pencil and paper

White candle

Candleholder

ADDITIONS OR SUBSTITUTIONS:
Orange paper for the planet Mercury, if both parties are misunderstanding. Or blue paper to represent your throat chakra if you feel that you are unable to communicate clearly.

Lavender oil, ruled by Mercury

Clear quartz crystal or gemstone for clarity

1. Cleanse your space and energetically purify your tools and ingredients, one at a time, with incense or another chosen method.

2. Create and write down your intention statement. Visualize a different outcome from communication that has gone awry in the past. Your statement might read, "I completely understand what's being spoken," or "I communicate clearly and with ease."

3. When drafting this sigil, envision a clear blue sky, or wind blowing through an open field of wild grass, anything that speaks "clarity" to you. Copy your sigil onto the orange or blue paper if you're choosing this variation.

4. Place the sigil under the candleholder and the candle in its holder. If using, place the quartz and bottle of lavender oil next to and touching the sigil and the candle.

5. Say your intention statement five times, light your candle, and then say "thank you."

6. Let the candle burn all the way down. If you need to leave home, extinguish the candle, and relight it when you return.

7. When the candle has burned, you can carry the quartz and lavender oil with you if you used them. You can also rub the lavender oil on the outside of your throat whenever you need a boost in clear communication.

TO HAVE A GREAT DATE

PURPOSE: To create an energy that allows you to have an amazing dating experience.

SETTING: Your ritual space at any time, but most effective on a Friday, the day ruled by Venus, preferably between sunrise and solar noon, or during the new moon

CASTING TIME: 15 minutes, plus time for the candle to burn completely

PRIMARY INGREDIENTS:
Incense, burner, and lighter/matches, or other purification tools

Pen/pencil and paper

Pink or red candle: pink for romance and red for passion

Candleholder

ADDITIONS OR SUBSTITUTIONS:
Red paper or pens, for passion and fun in your sigil, or pink paper or pens, for romance and intimacy

Rose incense, for the spell

Rose quartz or ruby gemstone

Small pouch of any color, but pink or red works great

1. Cleanse your space and energetically purify your tools and ingredients, one at a time, with incense or another chosen method.

2. Decide on and write down an intention statement for this spell. Rather than describe your ideal next date in detail, try a more open-ended approach, such as "I have an amazing dating life."

3. While drawing your sigil, you can play in your mind all the different attributes that would make a date amazing to you.

4. If using, copy your sigil now onto the red or pink paper, and light the rose incense.

5. Place your sigil underneath your candleholder and candle.

6. Set the ruby or rose quartz gemstone, if using, on your sigil, against the candleholder.

7. Repeat your intention statement six times. Light your candle and say "thank you."

8. Let the candle burn down. If you need to leave home, extinguish the candle, and relight it when you return. Once the candle has finished burning, take your sigil and fold it so that it will fit into the pouch, if you have chosen to use one.

9. While saying your intention statement one more time, place the sigil into your pouch, and add the gemstone, if using. Carry the pouch, or just the sigil, with you as long as it feels active.

ENDING A RELATIONSHIP WITH COMPASSION AND GRACE

PURPOSE: To end any relationship in a way that supports the health and well-being of everyone involved.

SETTING: Your ritual space at any time, but most effective during the waning moon

CASTING TIME: 10 minutes

PRIMARY INGREDIENTS:
Incense, burner, and lighter/matches, or other purification tools

Pen/pencil and paper

Rose incense or room spray, for the spell

Fire-safe vessel

Glass of water, half full

Healthy growing plant

ADDITIONS OR SUBSTITUTIONS:
Amethyst and rose quartz gemstones

1. Cleanse your space and energetically purify your tools and ingredients, one at a time, with incense or another chosen method.

2. Draft your intention statement using language that centers on the completion of the current relationship, rather than on cutting all ties with somebody. This is one of the rare occasions where it is appropriate to use a person's name in a spell or sigil. Just make sure that your intention addresses the relationship rather than the character of the other individual, like "I am bringing an end to my romantic relationship with _____."

3. As you create the sigil, try to evoke feelings of compassion for the other person while keeping your boundaries intact.

4. Now light the rose incense, and place it in the burner. Pass your sigil through the incense smoke or spray it. Do this eight times.

5. Place the sigil into the fire-safe vessel and burn it. Pour the ash into the glass of water. Drop your gemstones, if using, into the same glass of water.

6. While mentally and emotionally directing compassion and kindness toward the person in question through words, visualization, or thoughts, pour the glass of water, ashes, and gemstones into your plant. The next day, you can pick the gemstone out of the plant and carry it with you.

HEALING YOUR BROKEN HEART

PURPOSE: To find strength and closure at the end of a relationship. This spell will help speed up the healing process, as well as allow more ease with difficult emotions and better access to inner resources that give you strength.

SETTING: Your bathing area at any time, but most effective on a Friday, which is ruled by Venus, or during the first quarter moon

CASTING TIME: 30 minutes, plus the time it takes you to bathe or shower

PRIMARY INGREDIENTS:
Incense, burner, and lighter/matches, or other purification tools

Pen/pencil and paper

New bar of skin-safe soap

Carving utensil

1. Cleanse your space, in this case your bathing area, and energetically purify your tools and ingredients, one at a time, with incense or another chosen method.

2. Craft and draft your intention statement, remembering that this sigil will use healing energy to displace pain and sorrow. You're not removing pain but are allowing the positive energy in to supplant or replace it.

3. Draw your sigil. Include six dots in this sigil to represent the planet Venus. While doing so, try to remember how it feels when you're not suffering through heartbreak.

4. Carve your sigil onto the bar of soap. Visualize a healing green light being imbued into your design and the soap, radiating into everything it touches.

5. Take a shower or bath, applying the soap directly to your body.

6. If showering, envision the soap's healing green energy taking the place of any emotional pain, pushing it down the drain.

7. If taking a bath, imagine the same thing, but don't linger in the water. When finished, stand up in the tub, and imagine the drain sucking away the emotional pain. Then rinse yourself thoroughly with clean water.

8. Use your bar of soap whenever you shower or bathe, until the soap is gone. There is no need to re-carve the sigil unless you feel an urge to do so. That urge is your intuition telling you that the soap is no longer charged with the healing energy, and that perhaps you aren't yet fully healed.

RECONNECT WITH AN OLD FRIEND OR LOVER

PURPOSE: To reestablish communication or develop a deeper level of understanding with someone. This spell builds off the affection you've held in the past.

SETTING: Your work space at any time, but it is best performed on a Friday or during Venus retrograde, during which time loved ones from the past reemerge

CASTING TIME: 30 minutes

PRIMARY INGREDIENTS:
Incense, burner, and lighter/matches, or other purification tools

Pen/pencil and paper

Pink paper or pen/pencil, for copying the sigil

Glass jar, no lid

Rose petals for a past lover, or lavender herb for a past friend

Blue ribbon, long enough tie around the jar into a bow

ADDITIONS OR SUBSTITUTIONS:
Rose quartz and lapis lazuli gemstones

Picture of the intended person

Small pouch that you can carry with you

1. Cleanse your space and energetically purify your tools and ingredients, one at a time, with incense or another chosen method.

2. Call to mind a wonderful memory that captures what you value most about the person in question. Shifting that thought to the present, write a clear and straightforward statement, like "I have reconnected with _____."

3. Draft your sigil using the letter method and both of your names. If this approach isn't working for you, try another method while picturing the two of you willingly connected by a shimmery blue stream of energy.

4. Once your sigil feels complete, copy it onto the pink paper or in pink writing. Place your sigil into the jar. While stating your intention six times, sprinkle either the rose petals or lavender over the sigil in the jar. Add the rose quartz and lapis lazuli gemstones to the jar, if using. Tie the blue ribbon around the middle of the jar, and seal it into a bow.

5. Place the jar in a location where you can leave it safely for at least six days.

6. If at the end of the six days you still haven't reconnected with the person, take out some of the herbs and carry them with you. For greater effect, if you choose, use the pouch and carry the gemstones and the picture with you as well.

STRENGTHEN YOUR CONNECTION TO ANOTHER

PURPOSE: To reinforce a bond that you already have with a person or specific group of people in a way that benefits everyone involved. If even one person in the relationship doesn't gain from the new union, the spell will not work.

SETTING: Your work space at any time, but most effective just before or during a full moon

CASTING TIME: 20 minutes, plus time for the candle to burn completely

PRIMARY INGREDIENTS:
Incense, burner, and lighter/matches, or other purification tools

Pen/pencil and paper

Violet paper or violet drawing utensil, for copying the sigil

Printed photograph of you and the person or group. It's especially useful if you can find an image where everyone is pictured as happy or laughing. If necessary, two separate pictures taped together will work.

Dried violet flowers

Ground cloves

White candle and a candleholder

ADDITIONS OR SUBSTITUTIONS:
Amethyst gemstone

Purple candle instead of a white one

White gel pen to write on darker paper

1. Cleanse your space and energetically purify your tools and ingredients, one at a time, with incense or another chosen method.

2. Create and write your intention statement. For this spell, craft a statement that says something like "Our bond is strong and grows stronger every day." You can use your names if you like.

3. Using the method that most resonates with you, begin drafting your sigil. For inspiration, perhaps imagine yourself in the kind of connected relationship you would like to have. Try to capture any emotion that comes up visually within your sigil design.

4. Once your sigil feels complete, copy it onto the violet paper or with the violet pen or pencil. Layer your finished sigil on your photograph, and rest your candle in its holder on top of both. Use either a heat-safe holder or a photograph that you no longer need.

5. Sprinkle the violet flowers around the candle in a clockwise direction. Sprinkle a pinch or two of the clove powder on the candle. If you are using amethyst, place it beside your candleholder.

6. Say your intention statement three times, out loud. Light your candle, and offer a word of thanks.

7. Let the candle burn down all the way. If you need to leave home, extinguish the candle, and relight it when you return. Once the candle has burned, you can carry the amethyst stone, if you used one, with you.

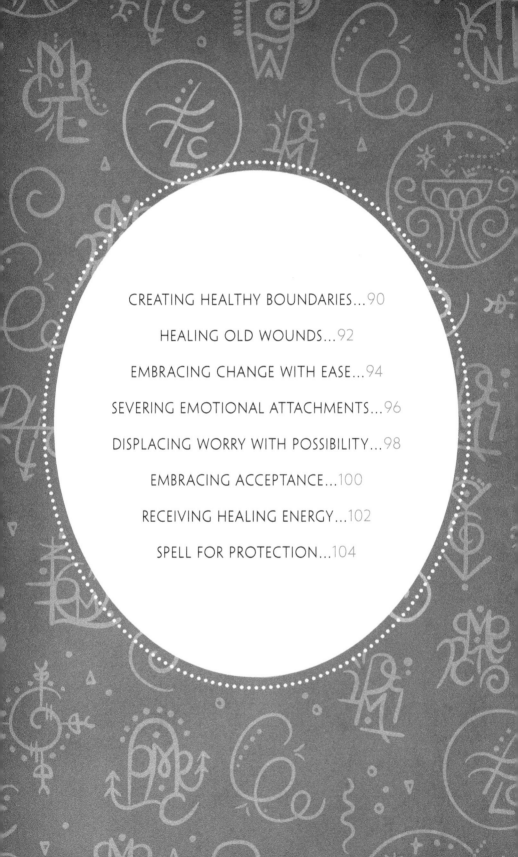

CHAPTER 6

Embrace Healing and Protection

Moving through this world can put a strain on the body and mind. Magic cannot replace physical practices. It won't stop bullets, mend a bone, or prevent another person from treating you cruelly. It's important to know when, in any given moment, to remove yourself from uncomfortable situations and to seek out a health professional.

But while magic cannot act as a physical shield, it can help to prevent hurt and to support you after you've been hurt. You can look to sigil magic to align the healing energy around you. It can help you calm your mind and access your intuition. You'll find spells in this chapter that create healthy boundaries and encourage emotional recovery. Sigil magic can also assist you in treating your body with care and gratitude, with spells for receiving healing energy, for releasing worry and stress, and for protecting yourself. Providing care for your mind and body will fuel your magical practice as well.

CREATING HEALTHY BOUNDARIES

PURPOSE: To help you establish healthy limitations between yourself and others so that you are not allowing yourself to be taken advantage of physically, emotionally, or energetically.

SETTING: Your ritual space at any time, but most effective on a Saturday, which is ruled by Saturn

CASTING TIME: 30 minutes

PRIMARY INGREDIENTS:
Incense, burner, and lighter/matches, or other purification tools

Black pen or pencil

Paper

Medium bowl sea salt

5 whole bay leaves

Scissors

ADDITIONS OR SUBSTITUTIONS:
Black salt instead of sea salt

Obsidian and rose quartz gemstones

1. Make sure you are in a location where you feel completely safe and protected.

2. Cleanse your space and energetically purify your tools and ingredients, one at a time, with incense or another chosen method.

3. Begin by writing down your intention statement, remembering that you are wording it positively to state that you're *creating* healthy, flexible boundaries rather than keeping something out. A sample could look like "I create healthy, flexible boundaries that are in my control."

4. Using a black writing utensil, draw a sigil small enough to fit flat inside the bowl of salt without being folded. When you feel the sigil is complete, draw a circle around it in a clockwise direction to symbolize boundaries.

5. Cut around your sigil and set it on top of the salt inside the bowl. In a clockwise direction, create a wall of bay leaves in the salt around your sigil. Make a complete circle with the leaves standing as tall as possible. Place the gemstones, if using, on top of your sigil.

6. Get in a comfortable position, and imagine a bright white light coming from your heart and radiating out to form a beautiful, shimmering sphere of energy surrounding you. Play with it and see how it moves and shimmers, but never breaks. Extend it outward, or bring it inward, always realizing that you are in control of this shield. Now imagine unwanted energies simply bouncing off the outside of your new boundary and returning themselves to their sender or dissipating completely.

7. While holding that vision, place the bowl in a secure spot and leave it there for as long as you need it.

HEALING OLD WOUNDS

PURPOSE: To bring in energy specifically to heal emotional pain from the past that may still be bothering you or preventing you from moving forward.

SETTING: Your ritual space, but most effective on a Sunday, which is ruled by the sun, representing health and vitality, or during the new moon

CASTING TIME: 20 minutes

PRIMARY INGREDIENTS:
Incense, burner, and lighter/matches, or other purification tools

Pen/pencil and paper

Yellow paper, for two copies of your sigil

Fire-safe bowl

Small pouch

ADDITIONS OR SUBSTITUTIONS:
Oil made especially for the purpose of healing; choose any formula that suits your practice

Sunstone or citrine

1. Cleanse your space and energetically purify your tools and ingredients, one at a time, with incense or another chosen method.

2. Write down your intention statement. Focus it specifically on an issue that's been emotionally charged for you for a long time. You could say something like "I release myself of _____ and make room for healing."

3. Decide on a sigil method that matches your mood. For inspiration, perhaps imagine yourself bathed in sunlight or warm soothing water. Make two copies of your finished sigil onto the yellow paper.

4. If using, place healing oil on your finger, or use your bare skin to trace a spiral on the first copy of your sigil, moving clockwise from the outside edge of the paper to the center of your design.

5. Rest your fire-safe bowl on top of that sigil. Arrange the pouch and any gemstones, if using, safely next to the bowl.

6. Take the second copy of your sigil, and set it aflame in the bowl while envisioning the fire burning away a cord between you and the past harm. Relight the sigil if the fire burns out before it is completely consumed by the fire.

7. Once the sigil is completely burned away, imagine a radiant yellow light coming from all directions into your mind and heart and saturating you with healing energy.

8. While still envisioning the yellow light, make sure the bowl is cool enough to touch, and move it aside. Take the sigil that was under the bowl and place it in the pouch while imagining the yellow light charging it with healing. Place the optional gemstone in with your sigil and close the pouch securely. Carry it with you whenever you need a surge of healing for your old wound.

EMBRACING CHANGE WITH EASE

PURPOSE: For calm and clarity when confronted by change, to help you remain open to a possible "yes" and find certainty in your "no." This ritual can also help you adjust to change.

SETTING: Your work space, most effective on a Wednesday or during the new moon

CASTING TIME: 20 minutes

PRIMARY INGREDIENTS:

Incense, burner, and lighter/matches, or other purification tools

Pen/pencil and paper

Orange paper or orange ink or pencil, for copying the sigil

Glass bowl

Lavender essential oil

Small glass pitcher of water with handle and spout

ADDITIONS OR SUBSTITUTIONS:

Botswana agate gemstone

1. Cleanse your space and energetically purify your tools and ingredients, one at a time, with incense or another chosen method.

2. Write down your intention statement; keep it in the present and positive. You could even recast the title of this spell as "I embrace change with ease."

3. Visualize a flowing stream or river, with a wide-open blue sky as inspiration. Breathe in deeply and exhale slowly. Begin drafting your sigil. Add five extra lines to the sigil anywhere you like, to represent the planet Mercury, which rules adaptability.

4. Once your sigil feels complete, copy it onto the orange paper or with orange ink. Place your sigil in the bottom of the empty glass bowl. If using, place the Botswana agate on top of your sigil. Drop five drops of lavender essential oil onto your sigil or agate.

5. Gently and slowly pour the water from the pitcher into the bowl while saying your intention five times. Stop pouring when you finish with the fifth repetition.

6. Reflect on managing changes in your life with as much ease as the water flowing from one vessel to another. Breathe in the smell of the lavender oil. Feel the emotions you have when you think of yourself handling change more smoothly.

7. Place the bowl in a location where it will not be disturbed, and let the water evaporate. Once the water has disappeared, take the optional gemstone out of the bowl and carry it to remind you of the spell's energy.

SEVERING EMOTIONAL ATTACHMENTS

PURPOSE: To help you separate yourself from emotional attachments that have become unhealthy or that prevent you from growing and transforming in your life. These could be to a person, place, physical item, or circumstance.

SETTING: A ritual space, most effective during the third quarter moon or on a Tuesday, which is ruled by Mars

CASTING TIME: 30 minutes

PRIMARY INGREDIENTS:

Incense, burner, and lighter/matches, or other purification tools

Pen/pencil and paper

Red paper and/or red pen or pencil, for copying the sigil

Freezer-safe plastic container or zip-top bag, nearly filled with water

Black pepper

Cayenne pepper

Garlic, powder or fresh

1. Cleanse your space and energetically purify your tools and ingredients, one at a time, with incense or another chosen method.

2. Decide on and draft an intention statement indicating that you are free from emotional attachments that no longer serve you. Be specific about the attachment you hope to sever.

3. Begin drafting your sigil. Envision severing a thread between you and the person, place, item, or situation. Let yourself experience any emotions that accompany the idea of disconnecting, like relief, sadness, or joy. Once your sigil feels complete, copy it onto the red paper or with the red pen. Add your name to the left side of the paper and the name or description of your attachment to the right side.

4. One at a time, mix the herbs into the water in the container. Black pepper and cayenne are both cutting herbs, and garlic is commanding and healing. Keep these attributes in your mind as you mix them.

5. While stating your intention statement, rip your sigil in half, separating the two names you wrote.

6. Place one half of the sigil in the container of water first and then the second half after. It's important to handle each side separately rather than together.

7. Seal your container, trusting the herbs and water to maintain a steady barrier between you and your attachment.

8. Set the container in the freezer and visualize that as it freezes, the cold is cooling off the emotions that were keeping you from moving on. Keep the spell in the freezer until you are free from the attachment, then discard it respectfully.

DISPLACING WORRY WITH POSSIBILITY

PURPOSE: To recalibrate your mindset to the possibilities and opportunities around you. This spell dislodges worries that cause self-doubt or cloud your judgment. It will not dampen the voice of inner warning in the face of possible harm. Note that if you have a diagnosed anxiety disorder, only use this spell to enhance your medical professional's advice and treatments. Never use a spell to replace any professional advice.

SETTING: Your ritual space, most effective just after sunrise

CASTING TIME: 15 minutes, plus time for the candle to burn completely

PRIMARY INGREDIENTS:
Incense, burner, and lighter/matches, or other purification tools

Pen/pencil and paper

Vanilla extract

White candle

Candleholder

Lavender herb, dried or fresh

A favorite piece of jewelry, something that you wear often.

ADDITIONS OR SUBSTITUTIONS:
If you don't wear jewelry, a clear or rose quartz crystal

1. Cleanse your space and energetically purify your tools and ingredients, one at a time, with incense or another chosen method.

2. Write your intention statement so that it brings something positive in, such as "I am in a perfect state of peace" or "I am full of possibility," rather than "removing worry."

3. While crafting your sigil, conjure inspiration by picturing yourself under a clear blue sky in a peaceful location where you feel safe and worry-free.

4. Once your sigil feels complete, place six drops of the vanilla extract in a clockwise circle around your sigil.

5. Put your sigil underneath the candle in the candleholder. Lay the jewelry, or crystals, between you and the candle. Allow them to touch the sigil. Sprinkle the lavender on and around the candle in a clockwise direction.

6. Take six slow deep breaths while holding your hands on either side of the candle. Keeping your hands where they are, say your intention statement six times. Light your candle with gratitude. Let the candle burn down. If you need to leave home, extinguish the candle, and relight it when you return.

7. When the candle has burned completely, tear your sigil in half to dispose of it. Wear your jewelry or carry the crystal wherever you go. Whenever you feel yourself starting to worry about something, touch your jewelry and state your intention in your mind. This jewelry will serve as a reminder for calm until it becomes a natural process.

EMBRACING ACCEPTANCE

PURPOSE: To release you from negative feelings about a circumstance you cannot change. This spell is not about agreement, but rather for finding acceptance or peace with a situation or person. It creates space for tolerance and opens you up to differences and imperfections.

SETTING: Your working area at any time. This spell is adaptable.

CASTING TIME: 15 minutes, plus time for the candle to burn completely

PRIMARY INGREDIENTS:
Incense, burner, and lighter/matches, or other purification tools

Pen/pencil and paper

Light blue or pink paper, for copying the sigil

Rose incense or room spray, for the spell

White candle

Candleholder

Pink calcite, rose quartz, or chrysoprase gemstone

Frankincense oil

ADDITIONS OR SUBSTITUTIONS:
Clear quartz crystal instead of the listed gemstones

Sunflower oil instead of frankincense

1. Cleanse your space and energetically purify your tools and ingredients, one at a time, with incense or another chosen method.

2. Write down your intention statement. A helpful framework might be "I allow ___ to be just as it is" or "I accept..."

3. While drawing your sigil, imagine a huge weight lifting from you once your resistance to accepting the situation is gone. Copy your sigil onto the light blue or light pink paper.

4. Taking a deep breath, light your rose incense and allow the smoke to engulf your sigil. Watch it surround the paper. If using room spray, spray the sigil directly. If the ink runs, allow it.

5. Position your sigil underneath the candle and holder, with the gemstone in front of the candle, touching both the sigil and the candleholder. Place six drops of the frankincense oil onto the candle.

6. Close your eyes a moment and picture the circumstance or person that you have been disagreeing with. Perhaps the image brings up a heaviness or discomfort. Feel that now.

7. Open your eyes and state your intention six times. Take a deep breath and light your candle, saying "thank you." Let the candle burn down completely. If you need to leave home, extinguish the candle, and relight it when you return.

8. Once the candle is completely burned, destroy your sigil by ripping it in half. Carry your gemstone with you, touching it as a reminder to accept the situation.

RECEIVING HEALING ENERGY

PURPOSE: To allow yourself to be free from any obstacles that may prevent you from receiving the healing energy around you. This spell will let you displace any metaphorical walls you have up that prevent healing from entering your mind, body, and spirit.

SETTING: This is a bath/shower spell. Once your sigil has been crafted, you can perform the remainder of the spell in your bathing area. It is most effective just after sunrise or on a full moon.

CASTING TIME: 30 minutes

PRIMARY INGREDIENTS:
Incense, burner, and lighter/matches, or other purification tools

Pen/pencil and paper

Yellow or green paper and/or yellow or green pen/pencil, for copying the sigil

Carnation flower petals and/or carnation oil

Sea salt

Citrine or emerald gemstone

Yellow or green cotton or linen cloth large enough to create a sachet; it will get wet, so make sure it is colorfast

Twine or string to close the sachet

ADDITIONS OR SUBSTITUTIONS:
Chrysoprase to replace citrine or emerald

Kosher or rock salt instead of sea salt

1. Cleanse your space and energetically purify your tools and ingredients, one at a time, with incense or another chosen method.

2. Write out your intention. Although this spell uses removal magic to address obstacles, your statement should seek out affirming words like "I receive all healing that is truly beneficial to me."

3. Using the method that most resonates with you, begin drafting your sigil. Inspire your creation with healing music or incense. Once your sigil feels complete, copy it onto the yellow or green paper.

4. Place the sigil, carnation petals and/or oil, salt, and gemstone on the cloth. Pull up the sides and corners to create a sachet and tie it closed with the twine or string.

5. Fill your bathtub with warm to hot water. Imagine an energetic yellow or green light coming from your tap. Place the sachet into the tub, and if you like, add some of the carnation oil to the water before bathing.

6. If you have chosen to shower instead, imagine the same energy coming from the water, and step into the shower. Hold the sachet over your head as healing water pours down on you.

7. Finish your bath or shower as you normally would, then discard your sigil and herbs with gratitude and respect.

SPELL FOR PROTECTION

PURPOSE: To create a barrier that protects you from unwanted external energies.

SETTING: Your ritual space at any time, but most effective on a Saturday, which represents boundaries, and during the full moon, which is a spell strengthener

CASTING TIME: 30 minutes, plus time for the candle to burn completely

PRIMARY INGREDIENTS:
Incense, burner, and lighter/matches, or other purification tools

Black pen/pencil

Paper

Black or brown candle

Candleholder

Sea salt

Mortar and pestle

African violet dried flowers

Star anise or aniseed

Cumin

Small pouch to hold ingredients

ADDITIONS OR SUBSTITUTIONS:
Hematite gemstone

White candle if another color is unavailable

1. Cleanse your space and energetically purify your tools and ingredients, one at a time, with incense or another chosen method.

2. Write down your intention. You can craft something general like "I am protected" or you can be more specific about the areas where you need protection.

3. Visualize a solid sphere of iron around you that you control. Work with this shield; imagine it impenetrable from the outside, but completely comfortable and transparent from the inside. Create a sigil with the black writing utensil that captures this feeling. Then draw a circle around your sigil in a clockwise direction.

4. Place the candle in its holder and on top of the completed sigil.

5. Sprinkle a circle of salt in a clockwise direction around the candle. In the mortar, combine additional salt, African violet, star anise, and cumin. As you are envisioning your new shield around you, use the pestle to break up and mix them thoroughly. Star anise can be hard to break apart; it's okay if it stays in large pieces. Sprinkle a pinch or two of this mixture onto your candle.

6. While speaking your intention statement, light your candle with thanks. Arrange the herb mixture, pouch, and gemstone, if using, next to the candle as it burns down. If you need to leave home, extinguish the candle, and relight it, imagining your shield again, when you return.

7. When the candle has finished burning, combine your sigil, the remaining herbs, and the optional hematite in the pouch. Visualize again the solid shield around you as you do this. Close the pouch and carry it with you whenever you like.

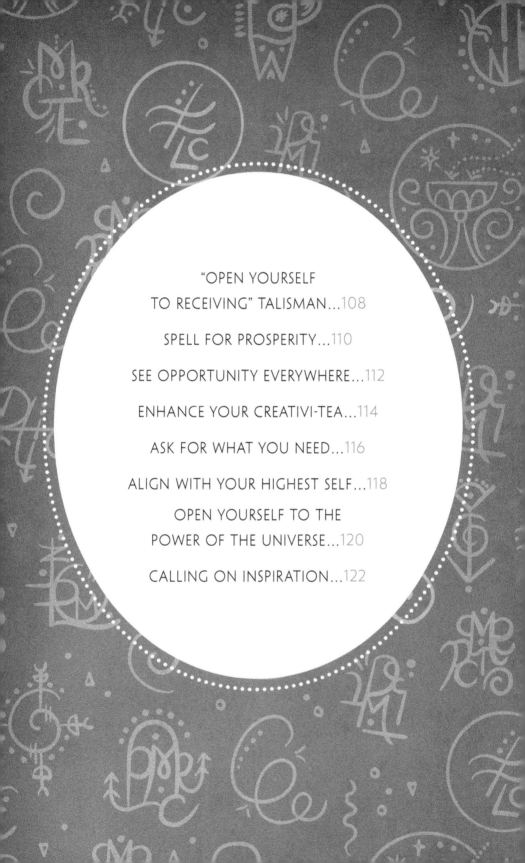

CHAPTER 7

Stay Open to Inspiration and Abundance

Inspiration and abundance can lead you on a path to fulfillment. Abundance speaks to what nourishes your person, while inspiration describes what fuels your creativity. Reaching fulfillment, however that feels to you, begins with a mindset that opens you up to possibilities and allows you to notice and receive what's around you.

In this chapter, the sigil magic draws in possibility and opportunity. It can help you shift your point of view so that you can see what's already in front of you. And it can allow you to gain enough courage to take action when opportunity arises.

The spells in this chapter are geared toward creating openness to the universe, as well as bringing in general prosperity, creativity, and opportunity. The sigil magic in this chapter will help you align with your highest self, find your creativity, and feel comfortable asking for what you need.

By engaging in these spells, you will be accessing magic that corresponds with your definition of fulfillment, enhancing *your* life and practice.

"OPEN YOURSELF TO RECEIVING" TALISMAN

PURPOSE: To create a talisman that provides you with continual magic, enhancing your energies to receive and channel the abundance that surrounds you.

SETTING: A safe location that is in view of the open sky during the new moon. It could be outside or on a windowsill.

CASTING TIME: 15 minutes to perform this spell, and 24 hours for charging the talisman

PRIMARY INGREDIENTS:
Incense, burner, and lighter/matches, or other purification tools

Pen/pencil and paper

Glass or ceramic bowl

Clear quartz crystal point

Silver charm that represents openness, such as a cup, an incomplete circle, or a horseshoe charm that faces upward

Gardenia petals, fresh or dried

ADDITIONS OR SUBSTITUTIONS:
Rainbow moonstone

1. Cleanse your space and energetically purify your tools and ingredients, one at a time, with incense or another chosen method.

2. Write an intention statement that reflects your *openness to receiving*. Keep in mind that moderation and specificity can be key when it comes to abundance, that too much of anything can become harmful. You could say something like "I am open to receiving all abundance that is desirable to me."

3. Design a sigil that reflects openness. Consider using the symbol method to extend your scope beyond the limited shapes of letters. If another approach is calling you, however, it's important that you follow that intuition.

4. Place your sigil into the bottom of the bowl. Set your quartz point on top of your sigil so that the point will be aiming inward toward the room for the full 24 hours that it will be charging. Lay the charm you have chosen at the end of the quartz crystal, and on top of the sigil, so that the open part of the charm is facing the crystal point. If you are including moonstone, position this at the other end of the quartz.

5. Sprinkle the gardenia petals into the bowl. Put the bowl in a place with a sky view where it won't be disturbed for 24 hours. After a full day has passed, you may take the charm, which is now a talisman, and wear it or carry it on your person.

SPELL FOR PROSPERITY

PURPOSE: To bring prosperity, whether it be material, emotional, romantic, intellectual, financial, social, or professional, into your life by allowing you to attract and receive it. Try not to limit the type that you're willing to receive.

SETTING: Your ritual space, most effective during a full moon, or at solar noon on a Sunday

CASTING TIME: 15 minutes, plus time for the candle to burn completely

PRIMARY INGREDIENTS:
Incense, burner, and lighter/matches, or other purification tools

Pen/pencil and paper

Yellow paper or yellow pen/pencil, for copying the sigil

Shallow heat-safe bowl, with sand to hold the candle

Yellow or gold candle

Pyrite gemstone

6 or 8 coins, real or symbolic

Nutmeg

ADDITIONS OR SUBSTITUTIONS:
Uncooked grains, symbols of prosperity

1. Cleanse your space and energetically purify your tools and ingredients, one at a time, with incense or another chosen method.

2. Write your intention in a way that opens you up to all forms of prosperity. You might say something like "I am receiving all forms of prosperity."

3. Using any method you like, design your sigil. For inspiration, perhaps imagine yourself surrounded by anything and everything that you truly desire. Once your sigil feels complete, copy it onto yellow paper.

4. Lay your sigil in the bottom of the bowl. Pour the sand or soil on top of the sigil. Set the candle in the middle of the bowl. Place the pyrite between you and the candle inside the bowl. Arrange the coins so that they touch the pyrite and each other in a semicircle around the candle. Make sure that the open end of the circle faces away from you.

5. Sprinkle the nutmeg all over the candle, soil, coins, and pyrite. If using, sprinkle a generous amount of grains over your ritual items.

6. Say your intention statement six or eight times. Light your candle and say "thank you."

7. Let the candle burn down completely. If you need to leave home, extinguish the candle, and relight it when you return. Once the candle is burned out, carry the pyrite with you, and safely burn your sigil to dispose of it.

SEE OPPORTUNITY EVERYWHERE

PURPOSE: To help you identify possibilities in everyday life so that you may choose to make the most of them. While the "Open Yourself to Receiving" Talisman (page 108) works by enhancing your energies to open you up to abundance, this spell operates by clearing your "vision" to see possibility that you might not currently notice.

SETTING: Your ritual space at solar noon or during a full moon

CASTING TIME: 20 minutes, plus time for the candle to burn completely

PRIMARY INGREDIENTS:

Incense, burner, and lighter/matches, or other purification tools

Pen/pencil and paper

Dinner-size plate

Pair of reading glasses that you won't need to wear while casting the spell

Gold-colored key charm

Eyebright herb, dried, fresh, or powdered

White candle

Candleholder

ADDITIONS OR SUBSTITUTIONS:

Printed image or drawing of eyeglasses if you don't have a pair to spare

Real key that you no longer use if you don't have a key charm

1. Cleanse your space and energetically purify your tools and ingredients, one at a time, with incense or another chosen method.

2. Write your intention statement. When wording this intention, assume that opportunity already surrounds you, but that you may not be seeing it clearly. You could say something like "I see all opportunities that come my way" rather than "Opportunity comes my way."

3. Using the method that most resonates with you, begin drafting your sigil. Imagine yourself placing a pair of glasses over your eyes. When you do, you bring into focus a vision of your hand holding a bright golden key, with an endless number of doors for you to choose from.

4. Lay the finished sigil onto the plate, and arrange the glasses touching the sigil, so that they are looking away from you and open. Set the key in the line of sight of the glasses, also touching the sigil. Sprinkle the eyebright herb over the glasses and part of the sigil, but not the key.

5. Place the candleholder with the candle on the plate to the side of the glasses and key as if it were a torch to light your key clearly. Sprinkle another pinch of the eyebright onto the candle.

6. State your intention once, and light your candle, finishing with a "thank you."

7. Let the candle burn down. If you need to leave home, extinguish the candle, and relight it when you return. You may clean and wear your glasses or key charm once the candle has burned down.

ENHANCE YOUR CREATIVI-TEA

PURPOSE: To create a magical tea that helps you get through a creative slump. This ritual removes blockages by actively moving creative energy through your space.

SETTING: In a kitchen or other space where you can boil water, at any time, but most effective between sunrise and solar noon

CASTING TIME: 15 minutes

PRIMARY INGREDIENTS:
Incense, burner, and lighter/matches, or other purification tools

Pen/pencil and paper

Orange paper or ink, for copying the sigil

Pot, teapot, or electric boiling kettle

1 cup water

Small bowl to combine herbs and tea

1 teaspoon green or rooibos tea

Sprinkle cinnamon

Few leaves lemongrass

1 clove

1 strand orange peel, dried or fresh

Tea cup or mug

Tea strainer

Optional sweetener of choice

1. Cleanse your space and energetically purify your tools and ingredients, one at a time, with incense or another chosen method.

2. Draft your intention statement as a simple declaration, like "Creativity," or with more detail and specificity like "My songwriting is enhanced and ongoing."

3. Draw your sigil while visualizing a bright orange light infusing itself into your mind. Consider adding another activity that might spur creativity before or while you draw, like listening to music or dancing. Once your sigil feels complete, copy it onto the orange paper.

4. In the kettle or pot, boil the water. As the water is coming to a boil, in a small bowl, mix the tea with the cinnamon, lemongrass, clove, and orange peel.

5. Place your sigil on a flat surface and sit the mug on top of it.

6. Place your tea mixture in the tea strainer and, once the water has come to a boil, pour it over the tea mixture into the mug, while saying your intention statement. Let the tea steep for 2 or 3 minutes before removing it from its place on the sigil. While the tea steeps, take in the aromas from it, and imagine what you'd like the enhanced creativity to help you accomplish.

7. Remove the strainer, sweeten to taste if you'd like, and enjoy your tea while thinking about creative endeavors you'd like to pursue. Destroy your sigil by ripping it in half.

ASK FOR WHAT YOU NEED

PURPOSE: To remove any energetic or mental obstacles, such as feeling like a burden or fearing loss of independence, that keep you from asking for what you need from people or the universe.

SETTING: A space with electricity or an open window, most effective on a Wednesday between solar noon and sunset

CASTING TIME: 30 minutes

PRIMARY INGREDIENTS:

Incense, burner, and lighter/matches, or other purification tools

Pen/pencil and paper

Blue paper or ink, for copying the sigil

Lapis lazuli and garnet gemstones

Small blue candle

Candleholder

"Mercury" purpose oil, or hyssop essential oil

Space on your wall where you can hang your sigil, and where the air of the fan can blow directly on it

Tape or string, for hanging the sigil

An electric floor, stand, or desk fan

ADDITIONS OR SUBSTITUTIONS:

If you don't have a fan, use either an open window or your breath

1. Cleanse your space and energetically purify your tools and ingredients, one at a time, with incense or another chosen method.

2. Write your intention statement. Even though you are removing obstacles, state your intention as if they have already been removed. It could look something like "I clearly and confidently ask for all that I need."

3. Draft your sigil using any method that calls to you. Once your sigil feels complete, copy it onto the blue paper and place it on a flat surface. Arrange both the lapis and garnet gemstones on top of the sigil, lapis on the left, garnet on the right.

4. Anoint the candle with the oil in an upward and counterclockwise direction from bottom to top. Set the candle and holder in the middle of your sigil. State your intention five times.

5. Light your candle and say "thank you." Let the candle burn for at least 5 minutes, all the while imagining yourself asking for what you need. This charges your gemstones.

6. Extinguish the candle, and remove your sigil from its location. Hang the sigil on the wall with string or tape, and turn on your fan. Imagine the air from the fan blowing away all that stops you from asking for what you need, clearing the energetic path between you and your sigil. You may also use an open window or your breath to blow on the sigil instead.

7. The spell is complete after a few minutes or when your intuition tells you. Turn off the fan, and rip the sigil in half to destroy it. Carry the gemstones with you as you wish.

ALIGN WITH YOUR HIGHEST SELF

PURPOSE: To create a tool and a communication method that taps into the truest, most attuned part of yourself. This can be useful if you're having a hard time making a decision. It connects you to the part of you that can make the decision more easily, the higher self or subconscious that isn't colored by the filters and opinions of your conscious decisions. The pendant you'll create acts as a pendulum to guide you in a particular direction. Use this pendulum only to communicate with your subconscious, not to communicate with external energies.

SETTING: Your ritual area at any time

CASTING TIME: 30 minutes

PRIMARY INGREDIENTS:

Incense, burner, and lighter/matches, or other purification tools

Pen/pencil and paper

Violet paper or violet ink or pencil, for copying the sigil

Labradorite gemstone pendant on a chain

ADDITIONS OR SUBSTITUTIONS:

Frankincense oil

Any gemstone pendant that you feel drawn to; use your intuition

1. Cleanse your space and energetically purify your tools and ingredients, one at a time, with incense or another chosen method.

2. Write your intention statement. It might be something like "I am aligned with my highest self."

3. Craft your sigil while keeping in mind your desire to be in alignment with your highest self. You might also draw something that *looks* aligned or in balance to you, like a visual pair. Once your sigil feels complete, copy it onto the violet paper.

4. Option to anoint your pendant with the oil. Then place the sigil in front of you, softening your gaze on it until it is out of focus. Continue until you see the sigil briefly disappear, flash an outline of light, or otherwise move or distort.

5. Hold the pendant over your sigil, with the chain in your dominant hand. Don't move; allow the pendant to become still.

6. Envision yourself somewhere you feel safe and peaceful. Imagine your highest self waiting there to guide you.

7. Ask as your first question, "Highest self, please show me the direction for yes." And allow the pendant to swing. That direction means yes.

8. Repeat the same question for "no" and "maybe," allowing the pendant to swing in whatever way it needs to.

9. Now that your pendulum can represent the responses from your highest self, and you know how to interpret them, ask any yes-or-no questions that you would like.

OPEN YOURSELF TO THE POWER OF THE UNIVERSE

PURPOSE: This spell works by opening a conduit to receive insight from the universe through your intuition. Use it when you feel disconnected, lonely, like you're making the wrong decisions, or when you can use some guidance about any part of your life.

SETTING: Your ritual space, most effective at night or during a new moon

CASTING TIME: 20 minutes

PRIMARY INGREDIENTS:
Incense, burner, and lighter/matches, or other purification tools

Pen/pencil and paper

Indigo paper or ink, for copying the sigil

Small bowl of water

Black candle

White candle

2 candleholders

Amethyst gemstone or crystal point

Borage herb, dried or fresh

Journal

ADDITIONS OR SUBSTITUTIONS:
Eyebright, instead of borage

Gardenia essential oil

High Priestess card from any tarot deck

1. Cleanse your space and energetically purify your tools and ingredients, one at a time, with incense or another chosen method.

2. Write your intention statement. Access to universal insight comes from trusting your intuition, so create a statement like "I trust my intuition completely at all times."

3. Using the method that most resonates with you, draft your sigil. Once your sigil feels complete, copy it onto the indigo paper, and sit the sigil underneath the bowl of water.

4. Set up the black candle in its holder on the left side of the bowl and the white candle on the right side. Place the amethyst between yourself and the bowl. If using the tarot card, place it underneath the amethyst.

5. Say your intention once, and light the black candle. Say "thank you." Repeat with the white candle.

6. Anoint your forehead with the gardenia oil, if using. Sprinkle some of the borage around the bowl in a clockwise direction. Try not to get any into the water.

7. Dim or turn off the lights, and get into a comfortable position that allows you to look into the bowl of water. While keeping your intention in mind, stare into the water. Let your gaze soften, and ask one question of the universe. Write down the first thing that comes to mind. Then begin to write the responses that you are hearing from the universe until you feel fulfilled or complete.

8. You can blow out the candle with gratitude when you are finished writing, and, if you like, use your sigil as a bookmark.

CALLING ON INSPIRATION

PURPOSE: To summon inspirational dreams when creativity and passion seem out of reach.

SETTING: Your sleeping area right before bedtime, most effective during the waxing moon

CASTING TIME: 15 minutes to perform the spell, plus time for the candle to burn completely, and a few minutes to finish it upon waking

PRIMARY INGREDIENTS:

Incense, burner, and lighter/matches, or other purification tools

Pen/pencil and paper

Light blue paper or pen/pencil, for copying the sigil

Orange candle

Candleholder

Glass of drinking water

Marigold flowers, dried or fresh

Journal

Small bowl

1. Cleanse your space and energetically purify your tools and ingredients, one at a time, with incense or another chosen method.

2. Write down your intention statement. You can use the word "inspiration," on its own, or be more specific like "I am inspired to . . ."

3. Draft your sigil. When connecting to a dream state, imagery can often be effective so you might consider the symbol method. But take the approach that feels right to you. Once complete, copy your sigil onto the light blue paper.

4. Place your sigil under the candleholder. Arrange the glass of drinking water so that it is touching the sigil and, ideally, the candleholder as well.

5. Circle the items with some of the marigold in a clockwise direction. State your intention five times, and light the candle, saying "thank you."

6. Place the journal and pen next to your bed, put the remaining marigold in the bowl, and set the bowl next to the journal.

7. Let the candle burn down. Then take the glass of drinking water and set it next to your bed. Before going to sleep, speak your intention statement into the glass.

8. If you wake up from a dream, immediately record it in your journal as best as you can.

9. If you wake for the day and don't remember dreaming, drink the glass of water. Then write down everything that comes to your mind.

10. To repeat the spell on other nights, refill the glass of water, leave it on the sigil for the day, and repeat steps 7 through 9 without the candle.

CHAPTER 8

Draw Strength from the Natural World

Connecting to the natural world is a magical experience, and many things, from immersing yourself in the outdoors to simply being present in the here and now, can create that connection.

As a magic user, establishing that link to nature is important in order to draw strength for spells, as well as for the daily routines in your life. That bond allows you to replace spent energy with the healing energy of nature. Think of this chapter as a cyclical practice to recharge your energetic batteries.

Another benefit to studying nature's cycles and practicing magic that celebrates them is that you will become more aware of the everyday phases in life and how they affect you personally. This enhances both your magic and your experience day-to-day. The spells in this chapter encourage this link with, and awareness of, nature's cycles. They'll help you tap into each of the four seasons, the full and new moon, and your own solar return, also known as your birthday. You'll even find a spell that minimizes the unwanted effects of Mercury retrograde, which is a part of nature's cycle that can cause miscommunication, errors, and mistakes.

By using the magic in the following pages, you can make that vital connection with nature and draw on its strength when you need it.

SPRING EQUINOX–AIR

PURPOSE: To use the element of air to connect your energy with the spring equinox, also known as Ostara. This part of the earth's yearly cycle represents new beginnings, fertility, and growth. By celebrating and becoming more in tune with nature's festivals and cycles, you stand to gain intuition, patience, and empathy, among other things.

SETTING: Your ritual space on Ostara, either just after sunrise or at the exact time of the equinox

CASTING TIME: 15 minutes, plus time to eat a hard-boiled egg

PRIMARY INGREDIENTS:
Incense, burner, and lighter/matches, or other purification tools

Pen/pencil and paper

1 hard-boiled egg, shell on

Pink, green, or yellow felt pen, to draw on egg

ADDITIONS OR SUBSTITUTIONS:
Broom

1 plastic egg in place of a real one; it will need to open and close

Extra paper if you're choosing to use the plastic egg

1. Cleanse your space and energetically purify your tools and ingredients, one at a time, with incense or another chosen method.

2. When writing this statement, think of an intention that fits the theme of rebirth for the season, such as finding new love, getting a promotion, or growing in your spirituality. You can also look at a more open-ended purpose like connecting with the spring equinox in new ways, or for the first time.

3. Craft your sigil. Because you are using the element of air, the letter method works very well here because letters are under that element's purview.

4. Once you've cleansed your ritual space and tools, it's an Ostara tradition to sweep away the negativity from your magic area or your entire home. Travel with the broom in a counterclockwise direction around the area, and sweep the energy out through a door or archway. You are sweeping energy at this point, not necessarily dirt. This is an optional step.

5. Carefully copy your sigil onto the eggshell with the colored felt pens while holding your intention in your mind. Or fold up the sigil you created on paper, and place it inside the plastic egg, closing it again.

6. If you used a real egg, put it in the refrigerator until the next sunrise. Then remove it from the refrigerator, break off the shell while saying your intention, and eat the egg or offer it to your local wildlife or pet.

7. If you chose the plastic egg, place it on a windowsill until the next sunrise, then remove the sigil from the egg, rip it in half while saying your intention, and dispose of it with gratitude.

SUMMER SOLSTICE–FIRE

PURPOSE: Using the fire element as a connection to the summer solstice, also called Litha or midsummer. This link with the summer solstice can bring vitality, empowerment, joy, and abundance.

SETTING: This is a great spell to do outdoors, but your regular ritual space works well also. Perform this spell just before solar noon on Midsummer Day, or at the exact time of the solstice.

CASTING TIME: 15 minutes, plus time for the candle to burn completely and a few minutes the next day

PRIMARY INGREDIENTS:
Incense, burner, and lighter/matches, or other purification tools

Pen/pencil and paper

Red paper or ink, for copying the sigil

Yellow candle

Candleholder

Fire-safe bowl

ADDITIONS OR SUBSTITUTIONS:
Summer flowers or flowering plants, for your ritual space

1. Cleanse your space and energetically purify your tools and ingredients, one at a time, with incense or another chosen method.

2. Write an intention that is about bringing in self-empowerment, vitality, or joy. Or you can create something that generates abundance for your health or finances or connects you generally to the summer solstice.

3. While creating your sigil, sit in sunlight, if possible, or imagine yourself out in the sun feeling its energy surround you with life. Use any sigil-making method that feels right to you. When it's complete, copy your sigil onto the red paper, or use the red ink on white paper.

4. Set your candle on top of your sigil and place the empty bowl touching the candleholder. Decorate the working space with flowers, if you are using this variation.

5. Speak your intention with as much energy as possible. If you need to be quiet, visualize this step instead by imagining yourself yelling the words out to the whole universe and a bright yellow light bathing the words that flow from you.

6. Light your candle with gratitude. If you need to leave home, extinguish the candle, and relight it when you return. Once the candle burns down, remove the sigil and place it in the bowl. Set the bowl in the sunlight until solar noon the next day.

7. At solar noon, light your sigil on fire and place it back into the bowl. Repeat your intention as you watch the sigil burn. Take the ashes outside and release them to the sunlight, even if it's a rainy day, with a thankful heart.

AUTUMN EQUINOX–WATER

PURPOSE: To celebrate and connect you to the element of water as a source of thankfulness for the bounty of the autumn equinox, also known as Mabon, second harvest, or fall equinox. By embracing nature in this way, it will enhance your spells that create balance.

SETTING: Your kitchen or cooking area, just before sunset or at the exact time of the autumn equinox

CASTING TIME: 20 minutes, plus 10 minutes the next evening

PRIMARY INGREDIENTS:
Incense, burner, and lighter/matches, or other purification tools

Pen/pencil and paper

1 apple

Carving knife

Large bowl of water

ADDITIONS OR SUBSTITUTIONS:
Autumn leaves, to decorate your kitchen space

A small pumpkin instead of an apple

1. Cleanse your space and energetically purify your tools and ingredients, one at a time, with incense or another chosen method.

2. Write an intention statement about bringing in gratitude for what you already have. This was traditionally the time of year for the harvest, so people were grateful for the food. Or perhaps your statement could be about connecting with the element of water to balance an emotionally uncomfortable circumstance or relationship.

3. While drawing your sigil, visualize yourself floating in clear, calm water, completely safe and nurtured. Feel the embrace of it, the weightlessness, the release of tension or fear. Sense the water's coolness in contrast to the warmth of the autumn sun, and the balance they create in nature. Allow gratitude to fill your heart.

4. Once your sigil feels complete, use your knife to carve it into the apple or pumpkin.

5. If using, decorate your space near the bowl of water with the leaves. While saying your intention out loud, if possible, gently place the fruit into the bowl of water. Let it find its own position, and let it sit there.

6. At sunset the next day, repeat your intention while removing the apple from the water. Using the knife, cut the fruit in half across the sigil, destroying it.

7. You may eat the apple or pumpkin raw, or prepare it in a recipe. You could also gift it back to the earth by leaving it outside for the animals, or burying it to fertilize the soil. No matter which option you choose, keep gratitude in your heart for all that you already have.

WINTER SOLSTICE—EARTH

PURPOSE: Use the elements of earth and fire to embrace rest and recuperation as a normal part of life's cycle, connecting to the winter solstice, or yule. This is the time of year when the night is the longest. It's a time to perform magic that both lays to rest anything unpleasant from the past that is still affecting you and creates space to receive the positive things that are coming.

SETTING: Your ritual space on the winter solstice. Alternatively, if you have a fireplace, you can use that as your work area.

CASTING TIME: 30 minutes on the solstice, plus time for the candle to burn completely and 5 minutes the next day

PRIMARY INGREDIENTS:

Pine incense, burner, and lighter/matches

Green pen/pencil and any type of paper

Jar of soil or dirt, mostly full, with a lid

Red pen/pencil and any type of paper

White candle

Candleholder

Fire-safe bowl

ADDITIONS OR SUBSTITUTIONS:

Evergreen branches, mistletoe, or holly, to decorate your ritual space

1. Cleanse your space and energetically purify your tools and ingredients with the pine incense.

2. Using the green pen, representing the element of earth, make a list of everything that you would like to let go from the previous year. This part of the spell "lays to rest" everything on your list.

3. Once you feel this list is complete, burn it and place the ashes into the jar of dirt, burying them completely. Close the lid, and set the jar aside.

4. Write your intention statement. It should be about positive inclusion like "I bring learning into my life this coming year."

5. Using any method you like, create your sigil with the red pen or pencil, representing fire. Visualize the warmth and light of a roaring fireplace. Or sit in front of your own if you have one. Imagine how it will feel once your intention is realized.

6. Place the sigil underneath the candle and holder. Decorate your ritual space now, if you choose. State your intention, and light your candle with gratitude. If you need to leave home, extinguish the candle, and relight it when you return. Once the candle has burned down, remove the sigil and burn it in the bowl to destroy it.

7. The next day, after sunrise, empty the jar of soil back to the earth with your thanks.

NEW MOON MANIFESTATION

PURPOSE: To plant the seeds of your desires and goals for the upcoming lunar cycle. The moon's energy is so versatile that you can craft sigils corresponding to any aspect of your life that you wish to manifest. You can even incorporate multiple sigils into one spellcasting.

SETTING: Your ritual space or outdoors, during a new moon

CASTING TIME: 15 to 30 minutes, depending on the number of sigils you create

PRIMARY INGREDIENTS:

Incense, burner, and lighter/matches, or other purification tools

Pen/pencil and paper

Pot and soil to plant the seed

1 plant seed, any type

ADDITIONS OR SUBSTITUTIONS:

White gel pen and black paper, for copying the sigil

Place outdoors to plant your seed, instead of a pot

1. Cleanse your space and energetically purify your tools and ingredients, one at a time, with incense or another chosen method.

2. Decide on some goals you'd like to accomplish in the next twenty-eight days, and capture them in separate intention statements. Keep them focused enough that they can be well begun before the next new moon, such as "I manifest a new job" or "I have found my true love." Keep in mind that you'll need to create a corresponding sigil for each one. If you are new to the practice, limit yourself to five, saving any other desires for the next new moon.

3. As you create each sigil on separate pieces of paper, imagine each of your intentions already being fulfilled and how you might feel when they are. Make sure to remember which sigil belongs to which intention.

4. Once your sigils feel complete, copy each onto your black paper, if you choose to.

5. Bury your sigils in the pot of soil or outside, one at a time, while speaking each intention out loud. Plant your seed per its instructions into the pot of soil and sigils. Feel the potential in the seed, and how the process of growth and manifestation occur naturally and easily. Imagine your desires manifesting this same way.

6. Set your plant in view of the sky, then move it the next day to a more permanent location where it can thrive in accordance with any seed care instructions.

FULL MOON FORGIVENESS

PURPOSE: To connect to the full moon's energies and thereby create peace through forgiveness and introspection. The spell is for forgiving oneself or another, not for obtaining forgiveness from someone else.

SETTING: Bath or shower area during the full moon

CASTING TIME: 10 minutes, plus the time it takes to bathe

PRIMARY INGREDIENTS:

Incense, burner, and lighter/matches, or other purification tools

Pen/pencil and several sheets of paper

Fire-safe bowl

ADDITIONS OR SUBSTITUTIONS:

Lavender essential oil or bath bomb

Washcloth, if showering and using essential oil

1. Cleanse your space and energetically purify your tools and ingredients, one at a time, with incense or another chosen method.

2. Create a list of wrongs and slights that still bother you, or regrets that you may have. If you feel that you have none, skip this step. Set it aside.

3. The intention statement for this spell should simple, present-tense, and about forgiveness, such as "I forgive (person's name)." Forgiveness doesn't mean you agree with the original behavior or that you give any kind of permission for it to happen again. It means that for your own health, you are letting go of your emotional attachment to that experience. If you have a feeling of regret or guilt about something, you may need to forgive yourself.

4. Craft your sigil using your favorite method.

5. Fill your tub or heat the water in your shower. Place the lavender oil or bath bomb in the tub at this time, if using. To use the oil in the shower, prepare a washcloth with the essential oil on it and place it in the corner of the shower. This will allow it to fill the air with the calming scent as the steam accumulates.

6. Place your sigil near the tub or shower, pause to focus on it, and state your intention. Begin bathing. Repeat your intention statement while allowing water to flow through your fingers over and over. Equate the water's movement to how your emotional attachment might "flow" away.

7. Once you're done with your shower or bath, burn your list and sigil in the fire-safe bowl. After both have completely burned, wash the ashes down the drain with gratitude.

YOUR SOLAR RETURN

PURPOSE: Happy birthday! This spell employs the element of fire to celebrate you with love and recognize your victories over the previous year. Enhancing this natural connection will generate a sense of self-love and confidence.

SETTING: Your ritual space, early on your birthday. If you can't do this spell on your birthday, pick a day close to it.

CASTING TIME: 20 minutes for the spell, plus the rest of the day to celebrate you

PRIMARY INGREDIENTS:

Incense, burner, and lighter/matches, or other purification tools

Pen/pencil and several sheets of paper

Yellow paper or pen/pencil, for copying the sigil

Copy of astrological birth chart, available free online

1 yellow or white birthday candle

Candleholder

Fire-safe bowl

1 beautifully wrapped gift from yourself, something you've really been wishing for

1. Cleanse your space and energetically purify your tools and ingredients, one at a time, with incense or another chosen method.

2. Create a list of your victories. Write as many down as you can think of: little ones, big ones, and everything in between. Feel the glow of accomplishment as you are writing.

3. Come up with an intention statement that lights you up. Try thinking of an attribute that you'd like to gift to yourself. It could even be a simple word like "joy," "love," or "confidence."

4. Design your sigil using any method that is joyful to you. When it's done, copy it onto the yellow paper.

5. Lay your astrological chart on your work surface, your sigil on top of that, and your candle and holder on top of your sigil.

6. Light your candle, and state your intention. Concentrate on the feeling of that intention being fulfilled, and read your entire victory list, out loud if possible. Be present with each one as you read it, absorbing the fact that these are all accomplishments you achieved. When you are done, state your intention one more time, and blow out your candle.

7. Use fire to destroy your sigil in the fire-safe bowl, and release the ashes with your thanks, however feels right to you. Open your gift to yourself, and spend the day any way that you please.

MINIMIZING MERCURY RETROGRADE

PURPOSE: To protect yourself and minimize some of the more challenging energies that occur during Mercury retrograde (see the introduction to chapter 8, page 125).

SETTING: Your ritual space, right before Mercury retrograde. If you miss the beginning, you can still do it during the retrograde.

CASTING TIME: 15 minutes, plus time for the candle to burn completely

PRIMARY INGREDIENTS:
Incense, burner, and lighter/matches, or other purification tools

Pen/pencil and paper

Orange candle

Carving tool, to carve the sigil into the candle

Candleholder

Fluorite gemstone, any color

Small pouch

ADDITIONS OR SUBSTITUTIONS:
If you have a fluorite pendant or charm, you can use that instead of the pouch and loose stone

"Mercury" purpose oil, a mix of essential oils and herbs associated with the planet

1. Cleanse your space and energetically purify your tools and ingredients, one at a time, with incense or another chosen method.

2. Retrograde energies are not all bad, so compose an intention that protects you only from the *unwanted* effects of Mercury retrograde. For example, you could write a statement like "I am protected from computer problems that may happen because of Mercury retrograde."

3. Design a sigil. As you work, envision a shield surrounding you. Mentally build a door within this protective sphere. At that door, picture an energetic force, like a guard at the gate. This force only lets in aspects of Mercury retrograde that are beneficial to you, leaving you protected from its unwanted attributes.

4. Once your sigil feels complete, carve a copy of it into your candle.

5. Put your sigil underneath the candleholder. If using, anoint your candle with the Mercury oil, starting from the middle of the candle and moving the oil toward each end of it in a straight line. Place it in its holder.

6. Place the stone and pouch next to the candleholder, touching both it and the sigil. Speak your intention and light your candle, saying "thank you." Let the candle burn down completely. If you need to leave home, extinguish the candle, and relight it when you return. Then place the gemstone into the pouch, while repeating your intention once again.

7. Carry your gemstone with you during this retrograde period only. Other retrogrades would require a repeat of the full spell, but you can use the same gemstone for each repetition. Destroy your sigil by tearing it in half and disposing of it with gratitude.

CHAPTER 9

Nourish Your Home and Everyday Life

Having an environment that nurtures your spirit and your magic is an important aspect of living a magical lifestyle. You and your practice are enhanced when you build a supportive environment that reflects who you truly are.

At every experience level, magic can be a way of helping out with the circumstances of everyday life, perhaps giving you a little more ease with any challenges you may face. It can serve as a kind of background energy, transforming the ways situations affect you and how you appreciate and interact with your environment. For example, one spell in this chapter can shift your daily viewpoint to prioritizing yourself without sacrificing others; another entirely different spell helps you declutter your environment. Other spells assist you in finding gratitude and joy, even when life seems challenging.

You'll also discover magic here that can inspire your decorating skills to create a more beautiful home, one that uses mirrors to help keep your environment invisible to prying eyes, and a spell that brings you energy when you feel exhausted. Take good care of your environment and your daily life, and magic will follow.

PRIORITIZING YOU

PURPOSE: To find a balance between selflessness and self-care such that you are always empowered and energized to maintain an equilibrium between the two.

SETTING: Your ritual space at any time you wish, but most effective during the first quarter moon

CASTING TIME: 30 minutes, plus time for the candle to burn completely

PRIMARY INGREDIENTS:

Incense, burner, and lighter/matches, or other purification tools

Pen/pencil and several sheets of paper

Small pouch

Rose quartz gemstone

Pink candle

White candle

2 candleholders

Small bowl of water

Lavender herb and rose petals

1. Cleanse your space and energetically purify your tools and ingredients, one at a time, with incense or another chosen method.

2. Write an intention statement that emphasizes balance between your needs and others'. Consider including a time frame, such as "I prioritize my self-care as much as I care for others every day."

3. Create your sigil using any method you like. Inspire yourself by imagining what life might look like if if you had the energy and time to balance everyone's needs, including your own.

4. When your sigil feels right to you, make two separate copies of it.

5. Place your pouch and gemstone in the middle of your work space and arrange your sigils on either side of them.

6. Set your candles in holders on top of the sigils, the pink on the left and the white on the right.

7. Put the bowl of water in a safe place where it can be left after the spell is complete. Sprinkle the rose petals and lavender over your work space.

8. Light the pink candle. This represents you and the idea that self-compassion can come first. State your intention clearly and with love. Now light the white candle, which represents your generous acts of giving. Speak your intention again with compassion and joy.

9. Let the candles burn down. If you need to leave home, extinguish then relight them. Then put one of the sigils, and some of the herbs, into the bowl of water. Leave it there until the water evaporates. Insert the other sigil and the gemstone into the pouch while repeating your intention. Carry it with you until you no longer feel that you need it. Then discard it with respect and gratitude.

BEAUTIFUL HEARTH AND HOME

PURPOSE: To bring you time, inspiration, and energy to create a magically beautiful home that supports your unique way of spellcasting and living.

SETTING: Your kitchen at any time, but most effective just after sunrise

CASTING TIME: 30 minutes

PRIMARY INGREDIENTS:

Incense, burner, and lighter/matches, or other purification tools

Pen/pencil and paper

Cutting knife and carving knife (they can be the same knife)

1 apple

Pot with water

Stove or hotplate

Lemon, orange, or lime, sliced

Cinnamon

Cloves

Vanilla extract

Wooden spoon

Journal

1. Cleanse your space and energetically purify your tools and ingredients, one at a time, with incense or another chosen method.

2. Write an intention statement to help you create whatever beauty will inspire you to live magically. Acknowledge if time, energy, or inspiration would let you establish this supportive environment. For example, "I find inspiration daily to create my magical home."

3. While creating a simple sigil that you can carve into an apple, visualize yourself finding, buying, and creating items to decorate your home. You may choose to incorporate symbols for these items into your sigil. Follow your instincts.

4. Carve a copy of your sigil into the apple skin. It doesn't have to be perfect.

5. Cut your apple in half horizontally, using the center of your sigil as the midpoint. If sliced correctly, the pattern at the core will look like a pentagram.

6. In your pot of water, combine the citrus slices, cinnamon, cloves, and vanilla. Bring them to a boil. Reduce heat to a low simmer. Add the apple halves.

7. Using your wooden spoon, stir the mixture clockwise while repeating your intention six times. Lay your spoon across the top of the simmering pot and take in the aroma.

8. Staying close to your pot, take out your journal and jot down any ideas that come to you to enhance your home and hearth.

9. Turn off your cooking mixture before it boils down or add more water if you need more time to brainstorm.

DECLUTTER YOUR LIFE

PURPOSE: To create a tool that will allow you to cut ties with clutter in your home, or anywhere else, by severing the energetic link that maintains attachments to items that no longer serve you.

SETTING: Your ritual space just after the full moon

CASTING TIME: 15 minutes, plus time for the candle to burn completely

PRIMARY INGREDIENTS:
Incense, burner, and lighter/matches, or other purification tools

Pen/pencil and paper

Red paper or ink, for copying the sigil

Candleholder

Red birthday candle

Amethyst crystal that has a point at one end, rather than a tumbled stone

9-inch piece cotton string or twine

Scissors

Fire-safe bowl

1. Cleanse your space and energetically purify your tools and ingredients, one at a time, with incense or another chosen method.

2. Write your intention statement while keeping in mind that you are cutting energetic attachments that you may not even be aware of, and that no longer serve you, not links to things that bring fond memories. Also, be firm by using words like "cut" or "sever," rather than "release" or "let go."

3. Design a sigil that captures a sense of space and freedom that will come once unwanted ties are undone between you and your clutter. When you feel your sigil is complete, copy it onto the red paper or with red ink.

4. Set your sigil underneath the candleholder and candle. Place the amethyst in front of the candle, touching the sigil. Say your intention nine times, out loud if possible. Light your candle.

5. Let it burn down completely. If you need to leave home, extinguish the candle, and relight it when you return. Then pick up the string, and state your intention again, imagining that it represents your unwanted link to clutter. Cut the string into two pieces. Take your sigil out from under the candle, and roll it up into a tube shape. Tie each piece of the string around your rolled-up sigil, one at either end. Burn the sigil in the fire-safe bowl. The sigil will come unrolled, but that's fine.

6. Your amethyst should now be primed to help cut attachments. Whenever you're ready, touch it to items you'd like to remove. Let the crystal give you the strength to release them. If you still feel linked to a possession, honor that feeling. It may be that it's meant to stay in your life for now.

INVISIBILITY MIRROR SPELL

PURPOSE: To create invisibility of the parts of your life that you don't want seen by others, such as your magical practice, ongoing spells, or magical items in your home. It could also work to keep secrets or to hide gifts you're not ready to give. Note that this is a type of ritual that acts on another person directly, asking their mind not to register the existence of whatever it is that you'd like to protect. There's a responsibility that comes with this type of magic. It means you'll need to be careful and very specific about both what you want to hide and from whom.

SETTING: Your ritual space during the new moon

CASTING TIME: 30 minutes

PRIMARY INGREDIENTS:

Incense, burner, and lighter/matches, or other purification tools

Pen/pencil and bright white paper for sigils

Scissors

6 small frameless mirrors

Tape or adhesive, to attach mirrors to cardboard

Cardboard box that represents your home, big and sturdy enough that you can attach one mirror each to all six sides

1. Cleanse your space and energetically purify your tools and ingredients, one at a time, with incense or another chosen method.

2. Write an intention statement that's as specific as possible. It could be something like "My magic is invisible to anyone who may wish it harm" or "My secret about _____ is hidden from _____." Think carefully about any exceptions or holes in the logic of your statement.

3. Draw your sigil, make six copies of the final result, and cut them to fit the back of each mirror.

4. Tape one sigil to the back of each mirror, with the sigil image hidden from view.

5. Attach one mirror to the inside wall of the cardboard box as you speak your intention. Make sure the glass side is touching the cardboard. Repeat for each side of the box, including the top and bottom.

6. Close your box and place it in a hidden location where it can stay. Check on it occasionally to make sure it's still intact, perhaps once a month on a new moon, or if you feel it has stopped working. Recharge your spell by repeating your intention whenever you feel it necessary.

GRATITUDE DURING DIFFICULTY

PURPOSE: To help start or reestablish a gratitude practice during challenging times. Participating in a regular gratitude practice has been found to have many mental and physical health benefits, and the happiness that results from it can benefit your magic practice.

SETTING: Your ritual space at any time, but most effective on a Thursday, because Jupiter rules both Thursday and gratitude

CASTING TIME: 15 to 30 minutes

PRIMARY INGREDIENTS:
Incense, burner, and lighter/matches, or other purification tools

Paper

Set of colored pens or pencils

Candleholder

White candle

Rosemary oil

Lapis lazuli gemstone

Rosemary sprig

Blank journal and pen

ADDITIONS OR SUBSTITUTIONS:
Amethyst or clear quartz, in place of lapis lazuli

1. Cleanse your space and energetically purify your tools and ingredients, one at a time, with incense or another chosen method.

2. Write an intention statement that motivates you to practice a daily thankfulness routine. For example, "I am inspired to find gratitude in everyday life."

3. Create a sigil that finds room and harmony for as many colored pens or pencils as possible. Imagine that each color you weave in represents something else for which you are grateful.

4. Put your completed sigil underneath the candleholder. Anoint the candle with the rosemary oil from top to bottom in a clockwise spiral and place it in the holder.

5. Place the gemstone in front of the holder, touching the sigil. Set the rosemary sprig on top of the journal and place it near the candle.

6. Repeat your intention three times, then light the candle while saying "thank you" out loud.

7. Pick up your journal and record everything you are grateful for. Continue to write until you are feeling full to the brim with happiness about your good fortune. Then extinguish the candle.

8. Return to the journal to add new lines when you are inspired. Use the rosemary or the sigil as a bookmark and place the stone nearby.

9. When times are difficult, revisit your list as a reminder of the good.

REST AND REFRESH FROM EXHAUSTION

PURPOSE: To use a visualization meditation spell to help calm, refresh, and reinvigorate yourself when you feel fatigued or burned out. The magic here works by creating a time-out to rest and revive. In contrast to Nurturing Your Energetic Fire (page 54), which lifts your energy as if you were drinking caffeine, this spell refreshes you with calm, like drinking chamomile tea, allowing your energy to replenish with rest.

SETTING: A comfortable place to sit or lie down. It works anytime but is best before going to sleep.

CASTING TIME: 30 minutes, but allow for the possibility that you will fall asleep

PRIMARY INGREDIENTS:

Lavender incense, burner, and lighter/matches, or lavender room spray

Pen/pencil and paper

Blue paper, for copying the sigil

Chamomile flowers, dried or fresh

Bowl of water

1. Cleanse your space and energetically purify your tools and ingredients, one at a time, by allowing lavender incense or room spray to waft over them thoroughly.

2. Create an intention statement that brings in a healing restful energy. You could say something like "I am completely refreshed" or "I allow my mind and body to rest."

3. Design a sigil using your preferred method. Once your sigil feels complete, copy it onto the blue paper.

4. Sprinkle as many chamomile flowers into the bowl of water as you like. Place the bowl of water near you and press the sigil into the water. It's fine if the ink starts to run. Close your eyes and speak your intention out loud. Take a slow deep breath in and let it out just as slowly.

5. Call to mind a refreshing and restorative scenario. It could be sitting by a calm lake watching the moonrise, a spiritual retreat, or a spa day with your best friend. If you find your mind wandering toward uncomfortable thoughts, simply observe this and restart your visualization. Continue the process until you notice every little bit of your body relaxing.

6. If you start to fall asleep, allow it. Come out of this meditation gently, by becoming aware of your surroundings through your other senses before slowly opening your eyes. When your eyes are fully open, say your intention again. Pluck your sigil from the bowl and rip it in half; dispose of your ingredients with thanks.

TIME TO NOURISH YOUR SPIRIT

PURPOSE: Your spirit and the ways that you sustain it are unique. So, rather than direct your attention to a one-size-fits-all type of nourishment, this spell focuses instead on creating time for you to practice feeding your spirit in your own way.

SETTING: Your ritual space while the moon is waxing or on a Sunday

CASTING TIME: 20 minutes

PRIMARY INGREDIENTS:
Incense, burner, and lighter/matches, or other purification tools

Pen/pencil and paper for several sigil copies

Scissors

Tape

Clock, big enough to attach a sigil

Jar of soil, with lid

ADDITIONS OR SUBSTITUTIONS:
Your cell phone, turned off, case removed

1. Cleanse your space and energetically purify your tools and ingredients, one at a time, with incense or another chosen method.

2. Write your intention in a positive, present-tense manner that allows for regular time to do a specific activity that nourishes your spirit: whatever makes you feel refreshed, whole, and at peace. If you're not sure exactly what feeds your soul, you can offer yourself time to explore what might.

3. Using the method that most resonates with you, create your sigil while envisioning yourself doing your chosen activity. Once your sigil feels complete, copy it two times, three if you're using the optional cell phone.

4. Cut one of them to fit the back of the clock, one to fit inside the jar of dirt, and, if using, one to fit inside your phone case. Adhere one of the sigils to the back of your clock so that the image is hidden from view. Do this while stating your intention three times.

5. Insert a sigil into your phone case, if using, then snuggle your phone back into its place while repeating your intention three times. Bury the third sigil facedown in the jar of dirt while speaking your intention three times. Close the lid.

6. Keep the clock where you normally might and the jar in a location where it won't be disturbed.

FINDING JOY IN THE CHAOS

PURPOSE: To create a spell jar that allows you access to the feeling of joy at any time, especially in circumstances where you might not normally be joyful.

SETTING: Your ritual space at any time, but most effective just after sunrise or on a Sunday

CASTING TIME: 30 minutes

PRIMARY INGREDIENTS:

Incense, burner, and lighter/matches, or other purification tools

Pen/pencil and paper

Yellow paper, for copying the sigil

1 small yellow or orange candle

Candleholder

Small glass bottle or jar, with lid

Pink Himalayan salt

Orange peel, dried

Calendula flower petals, dried

Peach moonstone chips

Honey, to fill the jar

1 cinnamon stick

ADDITIONS OR SUBSTITUTIONS:

Funnel or spoon to pour the honey into the jar

Gold glitter for beauty

1. Cleanse your space and energetically purify your tools and ingredients, one at a time, with incense or another chosen method.

2. Write an intention statement that expresses being able to feel joy in your life no matter the circumstances. Perhaps try something like "I am joyful at any time I choose."

3. Draw this sigil using your method of choice while visualizing yourself doing something that really lights you up and brings you happiness. Hold on to that image for as long as it takes to create your sigil. Once your sigil feels complete, copy it onto the yellow paper.

4. Light your candle in its holder; it will be used later, but for now let it bring light and cheer into your space.

5. Fold your sigil or roll it into a scroll so that it fits into the bottle, and place it there.

6. Layer the salt, orange peel, flower petals, moonstone chips, and glitter, if using, over the sigil in any order you like. As you add each ingredient, speak your intention into the jar with it.

7. Pour honey into the jar, leaving a little space for the cinnamon stick. As you pour, recall the joyful activity you drew on for inspiration while crafting the sigil, or bring a new one to mind.

8. Using the cinnamon stick, stir the ingredients into the honey in a clockwise manner while repeating your intention. When the items are combined, leave the cinnamon in the jar, and fasten the lid.

9. Using the burning candle, carefully melt wax around the closure to seal in the spell. This could take time; continue until the wax has covered the rim of the jar. Place the jar in a location where you will see it often.

A FINAL WORD

You are well on your way to being an expert in sigil magic. With practice and dedication, you will be able to create sigils quickly and effectively.

By using sigils in your everyday life, you have an opportunity to gain a better understanding of yourself and the world around you, because the creation of a sigil requires you to be in the present moment. For instance, creating a sigil asks you to visualize possibilities that you may never have imagined as a reality, rather than as a future prospect. In fact, you may already be noticing all the circumstances and distractions that have been preventing you from being present. The beginning of any transformation is first observing what it is that you'd like to change, and why it's important to you that you do that.

There are many ways that you can continue your journey. In practicing the spells in this book, you may have already begun to see the natural associations between the various ingredients and tools mentioned. You can also do your own research for planetary alignments, elemental associations, herbs, oils, magical color meanings, numerology, tarot, and everything else that can enhance your sigil work.

The more that you incorporate practical sigil magic into your daily life, the more you're likely to meet head-on any challenges that may arise. So, keep studying, keep practicing, and keep bringing your own unique magic to everything that you do.

GLOSSARY

BANISHING: A series of rituals that remove negative or unwanted energies from a space

CEREMONIAL MAGIC: Also known as high magic, this realm of magical practice uses invocations and spells to tap into the spirit world.

CHAKRAS: Energy points in your body that correspond and provide energy to seven discrete areas of the body

ENERGETIC EXCHANGE: A way to give energy to someone in exchange for a product or service, usually in the form of money, but bartering can be used also

EVOKE: To call upon a deity or being to work with the practitioner externally in ritual

INVOKE: To call upon a deity or entity to work from inside a magic user; a little like possession, but voluntary

LOGOGRAPH: A written or pictorial symbol that is used to represent an entire word

PANTHEON: The entire group of deities of a specific culture or religion

RETROGRADE: The appearance of a planet's backward motion in the sky

SOLAR NOON: The time of day where the sun is at its highest point in the sky, not usually synching with noon on a clock

SOLAR RETURN: Time of year where the sun returns to the same position that it was in at the exact birth of an individual; birthday

WANING: When the moon's light is decreasing in size from a full moon to dark

WAXING: When the moon's light is increasing in size from a dark moon to full

RESOURCES

PRINT

THE RULERSHIP BOOK by Rex E. Bills is a very comprehensive directory of astrological correspondences that will assist in the creation of your own sigil spells.

LIBER NULL & PSYCHONAUT: AN INTRODUCTION TO CHAOS MAGIC by Peter J. Carroll is the book that transformed Austin Osman Spare's sigil magic into what it is today and introduced chaos magic to the world.

LLEWELLYN'S ASTROLOGICAL CALENDAR has been published every year since 1932; this calendar contains a plethora of astrological information for each calendar day so you can time your spells.

THE THREE MAGICAL BOOKS OF SOLOMON: THE GREATER AND LESSER KEYS & THE TESTAMENT OF SOLOMON by Aleister Crowley, S. L. MacGregor Mathers, and F. C. Conybear is an all-inclusive book containing and discussing the commonly used Lesser and Greater Keys of Solomon, a different type of sigil magic.

ONLINE

SUNRISE-SUNSET.ORG tells you the exact times for sunrise, sunset, solar noon, and solar midnight for any location in the world.

ASTRODIENST.COM is a website where you can get free astrological charts, including your birth chart. There are paid options as well.

GALLERYOFMAGICK.COM is one of my favorite resources for sigil magic specifically.

REFERENCES

Beyer, Catherine. "What Is Chaos Magic?" Learn Religions. August 13, 2018. learnreligions.com/chaos-magic-95940.

——"Sigillum Dei Aemeth." Learn Religions. April 12, 2019. learnreligions.com/sigillum-dei-aemeth-96044.

Bills, Rex E. *The Rulership Book: A Directory of Astrological Correspondences.* Tempe: American Federation of Astrologers, 1991.

"Chaos Magick." Encyclopedia.com. Accessed January 24, 2022. encyclopedia.com/science/encyclopedias-almanacs-transcripts-and-maps/chaos-magick.

Compagni, Vittoria Perrone. "Heinrich Cornelius Agrippa von Nettesheim." Stanford Encyclopedia of Philosophy, Spring 2021 Edition. March 18, 2021. stanford.library.usyd.edu.au/archives/spr2021/entries/agrippa-nettesheim.

Feingold, M. "John Dee." Encyclopædia Britannica. Accessed November 27, 2021. britannica.com/biography/John-Dee.

"Heinrich Cornelius Agrippa von Nettesheim." Encyclopædia Britannica. Accessed September 10, 2021. britannica.com/biography/Heinrich -Cornelius-Agrippa-von-Nettesheim.

"Hunting Magic in Rock Art." Bradshaw Foundation. December 9, 2019. Bradshawfoundation.com/news/index.php?id=Hunting-magic-in-rock-art.

"Logogram." New World Encyclopedia. Accessed February 5, 2022. newworldencyclopedia.org/entry/Logogram.

Spare, Austin Osman. "Austin Osman Spare." Accessed February 13, 2022. austinspare.co.uk.

Wigington, Patti. "Ceremonial Magic." Learn Religions. November 29, 2017. learnreligions.com/ceremonial-magic-p2-2561878.

INDEX

ACKNOWLEDGMENTS

To my many magical and nonmagical teachers from the past for putting up with my incessant questioning; your patience was extraordinary.

To my partner in life for his enduring support and love. Thank you for playing in the sandbox with me.

To Alexis Sattler, editor extraordinaire, for her mad word skills that transformed this book into its own work of magic, as well as her cheerleading superpower that kept me inspired.

To Caryn Abramowitz, for asking all the right questions and brilliantly understanding the answers.

And to everyone who had a hand in creating this book whose names I don't know, thank you.

ABOUT THE AUTHOR

SHANNON C. CLARK began her journey into the magical arts in 1994 and now considers herself an eclectic pagan. With original teachings in ceremonial magic, she simultaneously worked in a metaphysical bookshop owned by a Wiccan high priestess and high priest, expanding the range of her magical knowledge and practice.

Her continued passion for all things occult led her into a lifelong study and practice in the mystical arts. She is the owner of SigilArtAndMagick.com, a resource website for magic users, and she is illustrator of the *Kingdom Within Tarot* deck and book set under the pen name Shannon ThornFeather.

CPSIA information can be obtained
at www.ICGtesting.com
Printed in the USA
JSHW060642270822
29778JS00001B/2